THE METROPOLITAN
TABERNACLE
ITS HISTORY & WORK

The Metropolitan Tabernacle
Its History & Work

Charles Spurgeon

CountedFaithful

THE METROPOLITAN TABERNACLE:
ITS HISTORY AND WORK

First published in 1876
This edition © Counted Faithful, 2020

COUNTED FAITHFUL
2 Drakewood Road
London SW16 5DT, UK

Website: http://www.countedfaithful.org

ISBN
Book: 978-1-78872-266-7
ePub: 978-1-78872-267-4
Kindle: 978-1-78872-268-1

Contents

Preface		7
1.	Earliest Times	9
2.	The First Two Pastors	18
3.	Benjamin Stinton	38
4.	John Gill	41
5.	John Rippon	54
6.	Deacon William Lepard	62
7.	Three Short Pastorates	74
8.	C H Spurgeon	81
9.	"Father" Olney	94
10.	Internal Condition in 1869	97
11.	The Almshouses	106
12.	The Pastors' College	110
13.	The Stockwell Orphanage	119
14.	The Colportage Association	131
15.	Other Institutions Connected with the Tabernacle	134

The Metropolitan Tabernacle

Preface

WHEN modest ministers submit their sermons to the press they usually place upon the title page the words "*Printed by Request.*" We might with emphatic truthfulness have pleaded this apology for the present narrative, for times without number friends from all parts of the world have said, "Have you no book which will tell us all about your work? Could you not give us some printed summary of the Tabernacle history?" Here it is, dear friends, and we hope it will satisfy your curiosity and deepen your kindly interest.

The best excuse for writing a history is that *there is something to tell*, and unless we are greatly mistaken the facts here placed on record are well worthy of being known. In us they have aroused fervent emotions of gratitude, and in putting them together our faith in God has been greatly established: we hope, therefore, that in some measure our readers will derive the same benefit. Strangers cannot be expected to feel an equal interest with ourselves, but our fellow members, our co-workers, our hundreds of generous helpers, and the large circle of our hearty sympathisers cannot read our summary of the Lord's dealings with us without stimulus and encouragement.

Our young people ought to be told by their fathers the wondrous things which God did in their day "and in the old time before them." Such things are forgotten if they are not every now and then rehearsed anew in the ears of fresh generations. "Why should the wonders he hath wrought be lost in silence and forgot?" We feel that we only discharge a duty to the present and coming generations when we use our pen for such a purpose.

Very graciously has the Lord dealt with us, and our own part of the long story is by no means the least bright with tokens of his goodness. Charged with egotism we may be, but if this be the penalty for declaring that "the Lord hath done great things for us; whereof we are glad," we will bear it with easy patience. The Baptist character of the book may trouble some thin-skinned readers of other denominations, but we appeal to their candour and ask them, if they were writing the story of a Methodist or Presbyterian church, would they think it needful, fitting, or truthful to suppress the peculiarities of the case? In all probability they would not have been less denominational than we have been, or if they had succeeded in being so, they would have robbed their record of half its value and all its interest. We do not expect in reading a life of Wesley to find his Arminianism and his Methodism left out, nor ought anyone to expect us to weed out Believers' Baptism and Calvinistic doctrine from the annals of a Particular Baptist church. *We are Calvinistic Baptists*, and have no desire to sail under false colours, neither are we ashamed of our principles: if we were, we would renounce them tomorrow. All controversial questions laid aside, dear reader, you will here see how our fathers struggled and suffered for liberty of conscience in former times, how their sons held fast the truths handed down to them, and in a measure how a church "upon whom the ends of the earth are come" still lives and flourishes by faith in the unseen God. How often prayer has been answered in our experience, and what great things faith has done for us, the latter part of this little book will show, and yet not all nor a hundredth part has been told or could be told.

We have taken passages verbatim from other works whenever they suited our purpose, and we have not mentioned the sources of our information, for such details are not needed in a mere popular manual. We end the matter in a word by saying that nothing here is original, but everything borrowed. How could it be otherwise in a history? Ours only is the setting; we could not make facts any more than jewellers can make diamonds.

May the reader's belief in prayer be increased, and his reliance upon God strengthened, as he reads our testimony, and should he unhappily be as yet unconverted, may he be led to believe in God, to rest in the sacrifice of Jesus, and cast in his lot with the people of God.

Brethren who have helped us so long, support our enterprises still by your prayers, your efforts, and your gifts, and so shall our Zion become increasingly a praise in the earth. To the Triune God be praise that for two centuries his mercy has surrounded this portion of his church, and that "his hand is stretched out still."

C H Spurgeon

1

Earliest Times

WHEN Knickerbocker commenced his famous history of New York, he felt it to be essential to begin with the Creation of the world. We labour under no such impression, and shall not therefore judge it needful to give a complete history of the Christian Church in the first ages in order to introduce our brief sketch of the Church in the Metropolitan Tabernacle. Still, a few historical memoranda as to the Christians commonly called Baptists, will not be out of place. Our own belief is that these people are the purest part of that sect which of old was everywhere spoken against, and we are convinced that they have, beyond their brethren, preserved the ordinances of the Lord Jesus as they were delivered unto the saints. We care very little for the "historical church" argument, but if there be anything in it at all, the plea ought not to be filched by the clients of Rome, but should be left to that community which all along has held by "One Lord, one faith, and one baptism." This body of believers has not been exalted into temporal power, or decorated with worldly rank, but it has dwelt for the most part in dens and caves of the earth, "destitute, afflicted, tormented," and so has proved itself of the house and lineage of the Crucified. The Church which most loudly claims the apostolical succession wears upon her brow more of the marks of Antichrist than of Christ; but the afflicted Anabaptists, in their past history, have had such fellowship with their suffering Lord, and have borne so pure a testimony, both to truth and freedom, that they need in nothing to be ashamed. Their very existence under the calumnies and persecutions which they have endured is a standing marvel, while their unflinching fidelity to the Scriptures as their sole rule of faith, and their adherence to the simplicity of gospel ordinances is a sure index of their Lord's presence among them.

It would not be impossible to show that the first Christians who dwelt in this land were of the same faith and order as the churches now called Baptists. The errors of the churches are all more or less modern, and those which have clustered around the ordinance of Baptism are by no means so venerable for age as some would have us suppose. The evidence supplied by ancient monuments and baptisteries, which still remain, would be conclusive in our favour were it not that upon this point the minds of men are not very open to argument. Foregone conclusions and established ecclesiastical arrangements are not easily shaken. Few men care to follow truth when she leads them without the camp, and calls them to take up their cross, and endure to be thought singular even by their fellow Christians. However, we are not now writing upon the question of believers' baptism, and are content to leave its discussion for another opportunity. We care more to be conformed to Scripture itself than to the oldest of usages. The moss of antiquity cannot command our veneration if it only garnishes error. The witness of churches is well enough, but "we have a more sure word of testimony" in the Bible itself.

We are content for present purposes to begin with a quotation from an adversary. That the (so-called) Anabaptists are no novelty in England is admitted by those least likely to manufacture ancient history for them. That rampant Ritualist, W J E Bennett, of Frome, in his book upon "*The Unity of the Church Broken*," says: "The historian Lingard tells us that there was a sect of fanatics who infested the north of Germany, called Puritans. Ussher calls them Waldenses; Spelman, Paulicians, (the same as Waldenses). They gained ground and spread all over England; they rejected all Romish ceremonies, denied the authority of the Pope, and more particularly *refused to baptise infants*. Thirty of them were put to death for their heretical doctrines near Oxford; but the remainder still held on to their opinions in private, until the time of Henry II (1158); and the historian Collier tells us that wherever this heresy prevailed – the churches were either scandalously neglected or pulled down, and *infants left un-baptised*."

We are obliged to Mr Bennett for this history which is in all respects authentic, and we take liberty to remark upon it, that the reign of Henry II is a period far more worthy of being called remote, than the reign of Henry VIII, and if the Baptists could trace their pedigree no further, the church of Thomas Cranmer could not afford to sneer at them as a modern sect. Concerning the poor persecuted people who are referred to in this extract, it seems that under Henry II they were treated with those tender mercies of the wicked which are so notoriously cruel. "They were apprehended and brought before a council of the clergy at Oxford. Being interrogated about their religion, their teacher, named Gerard, a man of learning, answered in their name, that they were Christians, and believed the doctrines of the apostles. Upon a more particular inquiry it was found that they denied several of the received doctrines of the Church, such as purgatory, prayers for the dead, and the invocation of saints; and refusing to abandon these damnable heresies, as they were called, they were condemned as incorrigible heretics, and delivered to the secular arm to be punished. The King, (Henry II), at the instigation of the clergy, commanded them to be branded with a red-hot iron on the forehead, to be whipped through the streets of Oxford, and, having their clothes cut short by their girdles, to be turned into the open fields, all persons being forbidden to afford them any shelter or relief, under the severest penalties. This cruel sentence was executed with its utmost rigour; and it being the depth of winter, all these unhappy persons perished with cold and hunger."

Induced, no doubt, to flee to this country from the Continent by the rumoured favour of Henry II to the Lollards, they found nothing of the hospitality which they expected; but for Jesus' sake were accounted the offscouring of all things. Little did their enemies dream that, instead of being stamped out, the (so-called) heresy of the Baptists would survive and increase until it should command a company of faithful adherents to be numbered by millions.

All along our history from Henry II to Henry VIII there are traces of the Anabaptists, who are usually mentioned either in connection with the Lollards, or as coming from Holland. Especial mention is made of their being more conspicuous when Anne of Cleves came to this country as the unhappy spouse of that choice defender of the faith, the eighth Harry. All along there must have been a great hive on the Continent of these "Reformers before the Reformation," for despite their being doomed to die almost as soon as they landed, they continued to invade this country to the annoyance of the priesthood and hierarchy, who knew by instinct the people who are their direst enemies, and whose tenets are diametrically opposed to their sway.

It may not be known to our readers that the Baptists have their own martyrology, and are in nothing behind the very first of the churches of Christ in sufferings endured for the truth's sake. A fine old volume in the Dutch language, illuminated with the most marvellous engravings, is in our possession. It is full of interesting details of brutal cruelty and heroic endurance. From it we have taken the story of Simon the Peddler, as a specimen of the firmness and endurance of the baptised believers in Flanders: one instance out of thousands: –

"About the year 1553, at Bergen-op-Zoon, in Brabant, there was a peddler named Simon, standing in the market selling his wares. The priests with their idol – the host – passing by, the said Simon dared not show the counterfeit god any divine honour; but following the testimony of God in the Holy Scriptures, he worshipped the Lord his God only, and served him alone. He was therefore seized by the advocates of the Romish Antichrist, and examined as to his faith. This he boldly confessed. He rejected infant baptism as a mere human invention, with all the commandments of men, holding fast the testimony of the Word of God; he was therefore condemned to death by the enemies of the truth. They led him outside the town, and for the testimony of Jesus committed him to the flames. The astonishment of the bystanders was greatly excited when they saw the remarkable boldness and steadfastness of this pious witness of God, who, through grace, thus obtained the crown of everlasting life.

"The bailiff, who procured his condemnation, on his return home from the execution, fell mortally sick, and was confined to his bed. In his suffering and sorrow he continually exclaimed, 'Oh, Simon, Simon!' The priests and monks sought to absolve him; but he would not be comforted. He speedily expired in despair, an instructive and memorable example to all tyrants and persecutors." [1]

During the Reformation and after it, the poor Anabaptists continued to be victims. Excesses had been committed by certain fifth-monarchy men who happened also to be Baptists, and under cover of putting down these wild fanatics, Motley tells us that "thousands and tens of thousands of virtuous, well-disposed men and women, who had as little sympathy with anabaptistical as with Roman depravity, were butchered in cold blood, under the sanguinary rule of Charles, in the Netherlands." The only stint allowed to persecution in the low countries was contained in a letter of Queen Dowager Mary of Hungary: "care being only taken that the provinces were not entirely depopulated." Luther and Zwingli, though themselves held to be heretics, were scarcely a whit behind the Papists in their rage against the Anabaptists, Zwingli especially uttering that pithy formula

---

1. A partial reprint of this volume was issued by the Hanserd-Knolly's Society in two volumes, entitled, "*A Martyrology of the Churches of Christ, commonly called Baptists, during the era of the Reformation.*"

Simon refusing to worship the host.

– "*Qui iterum mergit mergatur*," thereby counselling the drowning of all those who dared to immerse believers on profession of their faith. The time will probably arrive when history will be rewritten, and the maligned Baptists of Holland and Germany will be acquitted of all complicity with the ravings of the insane fanatics, and it will be proved that they were the advance-guard of the army of religious liberty, men who lived before their times, but whose influence might have saved the world centuries of floundering in the bog of semi-popery if they had but been allowed fair play. As it was, their views, like those of modern Baptists, so completely laid the axe at the root of all priestcraft and sacramentarianism, that violent opposition was aroused, and the two-edged sword of defamation and extirpation was set to its cruel work, and kept to it with a relentless perseverance never excelled, perhaps never equalled. All other sects may be in some degree borne with, but Baptists are utterly intolerable to priests and Popes; neither can despots and tyrants endure them.

We will leave the continental hive, to return to our brethren in England. Latimer, who could not speak too badly of the Baptists, nevertheless bears witness to their numbers and intrepidity. "Here I have to tell you what I heard of late, by the relation of a credible person and a worshipful man, of a town in this realm of England, that hath about five hundred heretics of this erroneous opinion in it. The Anabaptists that were burnt here, in divers towns of England (as I have heard of credible men, I saw them not myself), met their death even intrepid, as you will say, without any fear in the world. Well, let them go. There was, in the old times, another kind of poisoned heretics, that were called Donatists, and those heretics went to their execution as they should have gone to some jolly recreation and banquet." Latimer had before long to learn for himself where the power lay which enabled men to die so cheerfully. We do not wonder that he discovered a likeness between the Baptists and the Donatists, for quaint old Thomas Fuller draws at full length a parallel between the two, and concludes that the Baptists are only "the old Donatists new dipped." We can survive even such a comparison as that.

Bishop Burnet says that in the time of Edward VI Baptists became very numerous, and openly preached this doctrine, that "*children are Christ's without water,*" (*Luke 18:16*). Protestantism nominally flourished in the reign of Edward VI, but there were many un-Protestant doings. The use of the reformed liturgy was enforced by the pains and penalties of law. Ridley, himself a martyr in the next reign, was joined in a commission with Gardiner, afterwards notorious as a persecutor of Protestants, to root out Baptists. Among the "Articles of Visitation," issued by Ridley in his own diocese, in 1550, was the following: "Whether any of the Anabaptists' sect, and others, use notoriously any unlawful or private conventicles, wherein they do use doctrines or administration of sacraments, separating themselves from the rest of the parish?" It may be fairly gathered from this "article of visitation" that there were many Baptist churches in the kingdom at that time. This truth is also clear from the fact that the Duke of Northumberland advised that John Knox should be invited to England, and made a bishop, that he might aid in putting down the Baptists in Kent.

Marsden tells us that in the days of Elizabeth "the Anabaptists were the most numerous and for some time by far the most formidable opponents of the church. They are said to have existed in England since the early days of the Lollards."

In the year 1575 a most severe persecution was raised against the Anabaptists in London, ten of whom were condemned – eight ordered to be banished, and two to be executed. Mr Foxe, the eminent martyrologist, wrote an excellent Latin letter to the Queen, in which he observes: "That to punish with the flames the bodies of those who err rather from ignorance than obstinacy is cruel, and more like the Church of Rome than the mildness of the gospel. I do not write thus," says he, "from any bias to the indulgence of error; but to save the lives of men, being myself a man; and in hope that the offending parties may have an opportunity to repent and retract their mistakes." He then earnestly entreats that the fires of Smithfield may not be rekindled, but that some milder punishment might be inflicted upon them, to prevent, if possible, the destruction of their souls as well as their bodies. But his remonstrances were ineffectual. The Queen remained inflexible; and, though she constantly called him *Father Foxe*, she gave him a flat denial as to saving their lives, unless they would recant their dangerous errors. They both refusing to recant were burnt in Smithfield, July 22, 1575, to the great and lasting disgrace of the reign and character of Queen Elizabeth.

Neither from Elizabeth, James, or Charles I had our brethren any measure of favour. No treatment was thought too severe for them: even good men execrated them as heretics for whom the harshest measures were too gentle. Had it been possible to destroy this branch of the true vine, assuredly the readiest means were used without hindrance or scruple, and yet it not only lives on, but continues to bear fruit an hundredfold.

When Charles I was unable any longer to uphold Episcopacy, liberty of thought and freedom of speech were somewhat more common than before, and the Baptists increased very rapidly. Many of them were in Cromwell's army, and were the founders of not a few of our village churches. When these men were to the front doing such acceptable work for the Parliament, it was not likely that their brethren could be hunted down quite so freely as before. Accordingly we find that contentious divine, Daniel Featley, groaning heavily, because they were permitted to breathe, and between his pious groans recording for our information certain facts which are, at this juncture, peculiarly useful to us.

Dr Featley says: "This fire which in the reigns of Queen Elizabeth and King James, and our gracious sovereign [Charles I] till now was covered in England under the ashes; or if it brake out at any time, by the care of the ecclesiastical and civil magistrates, it was soon put out. But of late, since the unhappy distractions which our sins have brought upon us, the temporal sword being otherways employed, and the spiritual locked up fast in the scabbard, this sect among others has so far presumed upon the patience of the State, that it hath held weekly conventicles, re-baptised hundreds of men and women together in the twilight, in rivulets, and some arms of the Thames, and elsewhere, dipping them over head and ears. It hath printed divers pamphlets in defence of their heresy, yea, and challenged some of our preachers to disputation. Now although my bent has always been hitherto against the most dangerous enemy of our Church and State, the Jesuit, to extinguish such balls of wildfire as they have cast into the bosom of our Church; yet seeing this strange fire kindled in the neighbouring parishes, and many Nadabs and Abihus offering it on God's altar, I thought it my duty to cast the water of Siloam upon it to extinguish it." The waters of Siloam must have been strangely foul in Featley's days if his "Dippers Dipped" is to be regarded as a bucketful of the liquid.

The neighbouring region which was so sorely vexed with "strange fire" was the borough of Southwark, which is the region in which the church now meeting in the Metropolitan Tabernacle was born. We are not aware that any of its pastors, or indeed any Baptist pastor in the universe, ever set up for a priest, and therefore the Nadabs and Abihus must be looked for elsewhere, but Dr Featley no doubt intended the compliment for some of our immediate ancestors.

The fortunes of war brought a Presbyterian parliament into power, but this was very little more favourable to religious liberty than the dominancy of the Episcopalians; at least the Baptists did not find it so. Mr Edwards, a precious brother of the stern "true blue" school, told the magistrates that "they should execute some exemplary punishment upon some of the most notorious sectaries," and he charges the wicked Baptists with "dipping of persons in the cold water in winter, whereby persons fall sick." He kindly recommends the magistrates to follow the example of the Zurichers who drowned the dippers, and if this should not be feasible he urges that they should at least be proceeded against as rogues and vagabonds. No party at that time understood religious liberty to mean anything more than liberty for themselves. The despised Anabaptists and Quakers and Independents alone perceived that consciences are under no human rule, but owe allegiance to the Lord alone. Even the Puritans considered universal toleration to be extremely dangerous. All the powerful churches thought it right to repress heresy (so called) by the secular power. Things have gloriously altered now. No Presbyterian would now endorse a word of Edwards' bitterness. Thank God, the light has come, and Christian men heartily accord liberty to each other. The day we trust is not far distant when even the Episcopal body will allow us to bury our dead in the National graveyards, and will wish to escape from that connection with the State which is as injurious to itself as it is obnoxious to other churches.

Moved by the feeling that it was the duty of the state to keep men's consciences in proper order, the Parliament set to work to curb the wicked sectaries, and Dr Stoughton tells us: "By the Parliamentary ordinance of April, 1645, forbidding any person to preach who was not an ordained minister, in the Presbyterian, or some other reformed church – all Baptist ministers became exposed to molestation, they being accounted a sect, and not a church. A few months after the date of this law, the Baptists being pledged to a public controversy in London with Edmund Calamy, the Lord Mayor interfered to prevent the disputation – a circumstance which seems to show that, on the one hand, the Baptists were becoming a formidable body in London, and, on the other hand, that their fellow-citizens were highly exasperated against them." Or, say rather, that the Lord Mayor's views not being those of the Baptists, he feared the sturdy arguments which would be brought to bear upon his friends, and concluded that the wisest course he could take was to prevent the truth being heard. No Lord Mayor, or even king, has any right to forbid free public speech, and when in past ages an official has done so, it is no evidence that his fellow-citizens were of the same mind: Jack-in-office is often peculiarly anxious that the consciences of others should not be injured by hearing views different from his own.

We have now come to the margin of the actual personal history of our own church, without, we trust, having quite exhausted our reader's patience.

2
The First Two Pastors

FROM some one of the many Baptist assemblies which met in the borough of Southwark our church took its rise. Crosby says: "This people had formerly belonged to one of the most ancient congregations of the Baptists in London, but separated from them in the year 1652, for some practices which they judged disorderly, and kept together from that time as a distinct body." They appear to have met in private houses, or in such other buildings as were open to them. Their first pastor was

William Rider

whom Crosby mentions as a sufferer for conscience sake, but he is altogether unable to give any further particulars of his life, except that he published a small tract in vindication of the practice of laying on of hands on the baptised believers. The people were few in number, but had the reputation of being men of solid judgment, deep knowledge, and religious stability, and many of them were also in easy circumstances as to worldly goods. Oliver Cromwell was just at that time in the ascendant, and Blake's cannon were sweeping the Dutch from the seas, but the Presbyterian establishment ruled with a heavy hand, and Baptists were under a cloud. In the following year Cromwell was made Protector, the old parliament was sent about its business, and England enjoyed a large measure of liberty of conscience. Mr Henry Jessey was at that time minister of St George's Church, Southwark, and being a man of great weight, both as to character and learning, and also a Baptist, there is no doubt that Baptist views had a marvellous sway throughout the borough of Southwark and adjacent places. If it be asked how a parish minister became a Baptist, we reply, Jessey first preached against immersion, and by his own arguments converted himself to the views which he had opposed, practising for some time the dipping of children. Finding that many of his people repaired to Baptist conventicles, he studied the subject still further in order to be prepared to face these robbers of churches, and the result was that he was convinced of the Scriptural nature of their opinions and was immersed by Mr Hanserd Knollys. This circumstance tended greatly to strengthen the hands of the many Baptist churches on the south side of the river, and, no doubt, Mr Rider's people were partakers of the benefit. This would seem to have been a period of much religious heart-searching in which the ordinances of churches were tried by the Word of God, and men were determined to retain nothing which was not sanctioned by divine authority; hence there were many public disputes upon Baptism, and, in consequence, many became adherents of believers' immersion, and Baptist churches sprang up on all sides. Truth suffers nothing from free discussion, it is indeed the element in which it most freely exerts its power. We have personally known several instances in which sermons in defence of Infant Baptism have driven numbers to more Scriptural views, and we have felt that if Paedo-baptists will only preach upon the subject we shall have little to do but to remain quiet and reap the sure results. It is a dangerous subject for any to handle who wish their people to abide by the popular opinion on this matter.

How long William Rider exercised the ministerial office we are unable to tell, but our next record bears date 1668, when we are informed that, "the pastor having been dead for some time, they unanimously chose

Mr Benjamin Keach

to be their elder or pastor." Accordingly he was solemnly ordained with prayer and the laying on of hands in the year 1668, being in the 28th year of his age. As Keach was one of the most notable of the pastors of our church, we must diverge awhile from the beaten track to describe his sufferings for the truth's sake prior to his coming to London. He was continually engaged in preaching in the towns of Buckinghamshire, making Winslow his headquarters; and so well did the good cause flourish under his zealous labours, and those of others, that the government quartered dragoons in the district in order to put down unlawful meetings, and stamp out dissent. The amount of suffering which this involved the readers of the story of the Covenanting times in Scotland can readily imagine. A rough soldiery handle with little tenderness those whom they consider to be miserable fanatics. When the favourite court poet was lampooning these poor people,

Benjamin Keach

and ridiculing their claims to be guided by the Spirit of God, common soldiers of the cavalier order were not likely to be much under restraint in their behaviour to them. Thus sang Butler concerning the divine light, in lines which the court gallants loved to repeat, but which we cannot quote entire, for they verge on blasphemy:

> "For as of vagabonds we say,
>   That they are ne'er beside the way;
>   Whate'er men speak by this new light,
>   Still they are sure to be i' th' right.
>   A light that falls down from on high,
>   For spiritual trades to cozen by.
>   An *ignis fatuus* that bewitches
>   And leads men into pools and ditches,
>   To make them dip themselves, and sound
>   For Christendom in dirty pond;
>   To dive, like wildfowl, for salvation;
>   And fish to catch regeneration."

Keach was often in prison, and his meetings were frequently disturbed. On one occasion the troopers swore that they would kill the preacher, and having bound him, threw him on the ground, with the determination to trample him to death with their horses. Their design was frustrated by the interposition of the commanding officer, and Keach was tied across a horse, and taken off to jail. His little meeting-house in Winslow still stands, and we have obtained a drawing of it. It is down a tortuous, narrow lane, behind the houses, quite out of sight, and can only be discovered by making special enquiries.

Winslow Meeting House

In 1664, Mr Keach published a little book for the use of children, entitled, "*The Child's Instructor; or, a New and Easy Primer.*" This, one would think, must have been a harmless work enough, but his enemies did not think so. A weak cause is afraid of even the feeblest adversary. His little books were seized, and he himself was summoned to appear at the assizes at Aylesbury, October 8, 1664. The indictment against him will not, we trust, distress the reader: he need not dread the pollution of his mind or the depraving of his morals. Police reports are not nowadays quite so theological. Serious as the charges are, there are few men of our times who would think it any dishonour to be found guilty of them.

"Mr Keach being brought to the bar, the clerk said, Benjamin Keach, hear your charge. Thou art here indicted by the name of Benjamin Keach, of Winslow, in the county of Bucks, for that thou being a seditious, schismatic person, evilly and maliciously disposed and disaffected to his Majesty's government, and the government of the Church of England, didst maliciously and wickedly on the fifth of May, in the sixteenth year of the reign of our sovereign lord the King, write, print, and publish, or cause to be written, printed, and published, one seditious and venomous book entitled, '*The Child's Instructor; or, a New and Easy Primer*;' wherein are contained, by way of question and answer, these damnable positions, contrary to the Book of Common Prayer and the liturgy of the Church of England; that is to say, in one place you have thus written: –

"'*Q.* Who are the right subjects for baptism?

"'*A.* Believers, or godly men and women, who make profession of their faith and repentance.

"In another place you have maliciously and wickedly written these words: –

"'*Q.* How shall it go with the saints when Christ cometh?

"'*A.* Very well; it is the day they have longed for. Then shall they hear the sentence, "Come ye blessed of my Father, inherit the kingdom prepared for you;" and so shall they reign with Christ on the earth a thousand years, even on Mount Sion in the New Jerusalem.'

"In another place you have wickedly and maliciously written these plain English words: –

"'*Q.* Why may not infants be received into the Church now as they were under the law?

"'*A.* Because the fleshly seed is cast out. Though God under that dispensation did receive infants in a lineal way by generation; yet he that hath the key of David, that openeth and no man shutteth, and shutteth and no man openeth, hath shut up this way into the Church, and opened the door of regeneration, receiving in none now but true believers.

"'*Q.* What is the case of infants?

"'*A.* Infants that die are members of the kingdom of glory, though they be not members of the visible church.

"'*Q.* Do they, then, that bring in infants in a lineal way by generation, err from the way of truth?

"'*A.* Yea, they do; for they make not God's holy Word their rule, but do presume to open a door that Christ hath shut, and none ought to open.'"

The indictment appears to have contained an amusing clerical error, which charged Keach with writing, that the rest of the *devils* would be raised when the thousand years were ended. Many an indictment has been quashed for a far less serious mistake, but the judge would not listen to the objections of the jury, whom he bullied somewhat after the manner of Jeffries. He bade them bring him in guilty *with that exception*, and when this was done he pronounced the following sentence:

Judge. "Benjamin Keach, you are here convicted for writing, printing, and publishing a seditious and schismatical book, for which the court's judgment is this, and the court doth award: That you shall go to jail for a fortnight without bail or mainprize; and the next Saturday to stand upon the pillory at Aylesbury in the open market, from eleven o'clock till one, with a paper upon your head with this inscription: *For writing, printing, and publishing a schismatical book, entitled, The Child's Instructor; or, a New and Easy Primer.* And the next Thursday to stand, in the same manner and for the same time, in the market at Winslow; and then your book shall be openly burnt before your face by the common hangman, in disgrace of you and your doctrine. And you shall forfeit to the King's majesty the sum of twenty pounds, and shall remain in jail until you find sureties for your good behaviour, and for your appearance at the next assizes; then *to renounce your doctrines*, and make such public submission as shall be enjoined you. Take him away, keeper!"

Keach simply replied, "I hope I shall *never renounce* the truths which I have written in that book."

Benjamin Keach in the pillory.

The attempts made to obtain a pardon or a relaxation of this severe sentence were ineffectual; and the sheriff took care that everything should be punctually performed.

When he was brought to the pillory at Aylesbury, several of his religious friends and acquaintances accompanied him: and when they bemoaned his hard case and the injustice of his sufferings, he said with a cheerful countenance, "The cross is the way to the crown." His head and hands were no sooner placed in the pillory, but he began to address himself to the spectators, to this effect: – "Good people, I am not ashamed to stand here this day, with this paper on my head! My Lord Jesus was not ashamed to suffer on the cross for me; and it is for his cause that I am made a gazing-stock. Take notice, it is not for any wickedness that I stand here; but for writing and publishing those truths which the Spirit of the Lord hath revealed in the Holy Scriptures."

A clergyman that stood by could not forbear interrupting him, and said, "It is for writing and publishing *errors;* and you may now see what your errors have brought you to."

Mr Keach replied, "Sir, can you prove them errors?" but before the clergyman could return an answer he was attacked by some from among the people. One told him of his being pulled drunk out of a ditch: another upbraided him with being lately found drunk under a haycock. At this all the people fell to laughing, and turned their derision from the sufferer in the pillory to the drunken priest! insomuch that he hastened away with the utmost disgrace and shame. After the noise of this was over, the prisoner began to speak again, saying, "It is no new thing for servants of the Lord to suffer, and be made a gazing-stock; and you that are acquainted with the Scriptures know, that the way to the crown is by the cross. The apostle saith, that 'through much tribulation we must enter into the kingdom of heaven;' and Christ saith, 'He that is ashamed of me and my words, of him shall the Son of Man be ashamed, before my Father, and before his holy angels.'" He was frequently interrupted by the jailor, who told him that he must not speak, and that if he would not be silent, he must force him to it. After he had stood some time silent, getting one of his hands at liberty, he pulled his Bible out of his pocket, and held it up to the people; saying, "Take notice, the things which I have written and published, and for which I stand here this day, a spectacle to men and angels, are all contained in this book, as I could prove out of the same, if I had an opportunity."

At this the jailor interrupted him again, and with great anger enquired, who gave him the book; some said, his wife, who was near unto him, and frequently spake in vindication of her husband and the principles for which he suffered: but Mr Keach replied, and said that he took it out of his pocket. Upon this the jailor took it away from him, and fastened up his hand again. But it was almost impossible to keep him from speaking; for he soon began again, saying to this effect: "It seems I cannot be suffered to speak to the cause for which I stand here; neither could I be suffered the other day (on his trial, I suppose he meant), but it will plead its own innocency, when the strongest of its opposers shall be ashamed. I do not speak this out of prejudice to any person, but do sincerely desire that the Lord would convert them, and convince them of their errors, that their souls may be saved in the day of the Lord Jesus. Good people, the concernment of souls is very great! so great that Christ died for them: and truly a concernment for souls was that which moved me to write and publish those things for which I now suffer, and for which I could suffer far greater things than these. It concerns you, therefore, to be very careful; otherwise it will be very sad with you at the revelation of the Lord Jesus from heaven; for we must all appear before his tribunal." Here he was interrupted again, and forced to be silent for some time. But at length he ventured to speak again: saying, "I hope the Lord's people will not be discouraged at my suffering. Oh! did you but experience," says he, "the great love of God, and the excellencies that are in Him, it would make you willing to go through any sufferings for his sake. And I do account this the greatest honour that ever the Lord was pleased to confer upon me."

After this, he was not suffered to speak much more; for the sheriff came in a great rage, and said, if he would not be silent he should be *gagged*; and the officers were ordered to keep the people at a greater distance from him, though they declared they could not do it. At the end of a long silence he ventured again; "This," says he, "is one yoke of Christ, which I find by experience is easy to me, and a burden which he doth make light." But finding that he could not be suffered to speak, he kept silence until the whole two hours were expired; only uttering this sentence, "Blessed are they that are persecuted for righteousness' sake: for theirs is the kingdom of heaven." When the full time according to his sentence was expired, the under-keeper lifted up the board, and as soon as his head and hands were at liberty he blessed God with a loud voice for his great goodness unto him.

On the Saturday following, he stood in the same manner, and for the like time, at *Winslow*, the town where he had lived; and had his book *burnt before him*, according to the sentence. We cannot obtain any particulars of his behaviour there; and therefore thereon must be silent, not doubting but that it was with the same Christian spirit and courage as before.

The person who preserved this relation, being present, wrote down all he heard and saw, at the very instant; and makes this observation of

his suffering, namely, That he stood in the pillory full two hours to a minute, which was a more strict execution than ever he saw in town or country; that others always had their hands at liberty, but this godly man had his hands carefully kept in the holes, almost all the time, which must have rendered his punishment so much the more painful.

Mr Keach, after these afflictions, continued about four years in the country, preaching from place to place, both publicly and privately, as opportunities presented, being continually harassed and followed by his persecutors. His public trial and suffering rendered him more acceptable to the informers than other preachers, so that it was not likely he could enjoy any quiet settlement in those parts for the service of the church of Christ; and he, having not then taken upon him the charge of any special congregation, thought of removing to London, where he might have an opportunity of doing more good, herein obeying his Lord's counsel to flee to another city when persecuted where he was. Accordingly, he turned his effects into money, and set out with his wife and children for London, in the year 1668. In his journey up to town the coach was beset with high-waymen, who compelled all the passengers to come out of the vehicle, and then took from them all they could find of any value. Law-makers and law-breakers were very much alike in those days, so far as honest Christian men were concerned. This was no small trial, to be bereft of all that he had, and left to manage with a wife and three children in a strange place. Thus he came to London, without any money, and almost without acquaintance. However, a man of such a public character, and spotless conversation, was soon taken notice of; and the Baptists, who are as ready to acts of charity as any others, took care to supply his present necessities. He also joined with the rest of the passengers in suing the county, and so recovered the whole of his loss again in due time.

No doubt the fame of Keach's sufferings gave him the readier welcome in London among the Baptists, and he seems to have become the pastor of the late Mr Rider's congregation very speedily after his arrival. His persecutions were not at an end, but among a more populous community there were more means of escape than in the hamlets of Buckinghamshire. Meetings were held, though the numbers were limited, and the places kept as a secret among the members. Even then with all their care the church did not always meet in peace, and the brethren were seldom able to enjoy the singing of God's praises for fear of interruption from the authorities. Many such invasions of their peaceful gatherings did occur, and both the pastor and the leading members of his flock were made to suffer for the crime of worshipping God as their consciences dictated. We read that "being met together for religious worship in Jacob Street, in a private house down an alley, the churchwardens, with Mr Cook, a constable, came in and seized six persons, and had them before Justice Reading, who bound them over to appear at the quarter sessions. At another time they met together at the widow Colfe's house at Kennington, to celebrate the Lord's Supper. At the conclusion they sang a hymn, which soon brought the officers of the parish to them; but from the conveniency of a back door they all escaped except one, who, turning back again for something he had left behind, was apprehended and taken. He was carried before a justice of the peace, who committed him to prison, where he continued until some of his friends obtained bail for him. At the next quarter sessions he was fined, and the fine paid. The widow Colfe, at whose house they met, had a king's messenger sent to apprehend her; but being informed that she was nurse to one who lay sick of the small-pox, he departed with an oath, and sought no more after her. Mr Keach after this was sought for, by one of the king's messengers of the press, for printing a little book called *The Child's Instructor*. This book, as near as he could make it, was the same for which he was imprisoned and put into the pillory; the other being then not to be obtained, though he sought greatly after it. He was at this time tenant to that noted informer *Cook*, but not known to him by his name. The which, when he came to know, he told him that one of the king's messengers was in quest of him, and for his sake, as a tenant, he screened him. But at length he was taken up by a warrant, left by the said messenger with another man in their neighbourhood, and was carried before Justice Glover. The Justice being informed of an ancient gentleman of worth and credit (who was one of the members of Mr Keach's church, John Roberts, doctor of physic), sent for him; and when he came, asked him if he knew that man, pointing to Mr Keach. The doctor answered, Yes, very well. Then said the Justice, Will you be bound for him? Yes, replied the doctor, *body for body*. The doctor's bail was taken, Mr Keach was discharged; but in the issue, he was fined twenty pounds; the which he was obliged to pay, when others, under the like circumstances, escaped through the insufficiency of the bail that was generally taken in those times." The pastor evidently had a warm place in the hearts of his people, and they were willing to back him up when called before the great ones of the earth for Christ's sake. He must have endured much labour in those perilous times, for the church met in several sections at different houses, and the pastor hastened from one house to another, having thus to preach several times on each Sabbath, evading the watchful eyes of churchwardens, constables, and informers as best he could.

Benjamin Keach was one of the most useful preachers of his time, and built up the church of God with sound doctrine for thirty-six years. Having been in his very earliest days an Arminian, and having soon advanced to Calvinistic views, he preserved the balance in his preaching, and was never a member of that exclusive school which deems it to be unsound to persuade men to repent and believe. He was by no means so highly Calvinistic as his great successor, Dr Gill; but evidently held much the same views as are now advocated from the pulpit of the Tabernacle. Nor must it be supposed that he was incessantly preaching upon believers' Baptism, and other points of denominational peculiarity – his teaching was sweetly spiritual, intensely scriptural and full of Christ. Whoever else kept back the fundamental truths of our holy gospel, Benjamin Keach did not so.

During the time of an indulgence issued by Charles II the congregation erected a large meeting-house, capable of holding "near a thousand hearers," in Goat's Yard Passage, Fair Street, Horse-lie-down Southwark, and this is the first meeting-house actually set apart for divine worship of which we find our church possessed. The joy of being able to meet in quiet to worship God, the delight of all assembling as one church, must have been great indeed. One tries to imagine the cheerful salutations with which the brethren greeted each other when they all gathered in their meeting-house of timber, and worshipped without fear of molestation. The architecture was not gorgeous, nor were the fittings luxurious; but the Lord was there, and this made amends for all. In all probability there were no seats, for in those days most congregations stood, and pews are mentioned as extras which persons erected for themselves in after days, and looked upon as their own property. Mr Pike, in his excellent *"Sketches of Nonconformity in Southwark,"* thus speaks of this ancient house of prayer: – "The chapel in Southwark in Keach's time presented to the casual passenger anything but an un-picturesque appearance. Only little traffic in those days disturbed the surrounding quietness. In front of the meeting-house was a court, bounded by a brick wall; and a peep through the iron gates would have shown a pretty avenue of limes, leading to the principal entrance. In the earlier years of the present century an ancient Baptist was occasionally met with who remembered the spot as it originally existed." The chapel ultimately became metamorphosed into a cooperage, and part of the ground on which it stood was occupied by a blacksmith's forge. We attach no sacredness to places, and therefore do not regret that sites which became unsuitable through the advance of the population or the changes of trade have been abandoned for more suitable localities; yet we must confess we have looked for the spot in Fair Street with something of veneration, not for holy ground, but for holy memories which linger around it.

In these days Baptists are received into the family of Christian denominations without needing to defend their existence – at least this is the case where spiritual religion is possessed; but in those days our brethren were despised and sneered at, and had to fight for existence. Hence discussions and disputations were forced upon them, and able ministers had to become champions for the weaker brethren. Mr Keach was often engaged in controversy, and has the repute of having been one of the fairest and most moderate of disputants. He entered the lists with the renowned and holy Richard Baxter, and had the adroitness to turn Mr Baxter's writings against himself, showing that many of his reasonings rather supported than overthrew believers' baptism. Of this Baxter complains in a letter. "As I am writing this," says he, "the hawkers are crying under my window, *Mr Baxter's arguments for believers' baptism.*" Keach was also constrained to cross swords with Mr Burkitt, the esteemed author of "*The Practical Exposition of the New Testament.*" That gentleman was rector of Milden in Suffolk, and felt himself greatly ruffled by the coming of a Baptist minister to Lavingham, and yet more by the conversion and baptism of some of his flock. To put an end to this business he went down to the Baptist meeting with a company of his parishioners, and actually held the pulpit for two hours, and discoursed upon infant baptism. This unwarrantable intrusion produced a degree of warmth on both sides, but to Mr Burkitt must be conceded the pre-eminence in abuse. In a book which he afterwards issued, the rector used the following choice language: "Since the late general liberty, the *Anabaptists*, thinking themselves thereby let loose upon us, have dispersed themselves into several counties, endeavouring to draw away our people from us, by persuading them to renounce their first dedication to God in *baptism*, and to enter into their communion by way of *dipping*. One of their teaching disciples has set up in our neighbourhood for making proselytes, by *baptising* them in a nasty horse-pond, into which the filth of the adjacent stable occasionally flows, and out of which his deluded converts come forth with so much mud and filthiness upon them, that they rather resemble creatures arising out of the bottomless pit, than candidates of *holy baptism;* and all this before a promiscuous multitude, in the face of the sun." When so respectable a person as Mr Burkitt could condescend to give currency to such ridiculous falsehoods, it was time that he should be withstood by someone who could teach him better manners. His calumnies were answered by the testimonies of those present at the baptism, and his reasonings were confuted by Mr Keach in his book entitled "*The Rector Rectified.*" Christian courtesy would seem to have been at a discount when the titles of controversial pamphlets were of the kind indicated by the following – "*The Anabaptists washt and washt, and shrunk in the washing;*" and when texts were explained in violation of all reason, as for instance *Leviticus 11:17*, "The little owl, the cormorant, and the great owl," – "the little owl resembles the un-baptised child, the great owl the Anabaptist parent, and the cormorant betwixt them the wide-throated preacher that divides child from parent, dives into them and swallows their souls." Mr Keach had his hands full of disputes with Flavel and men of less note, but he deplored rather than delighted in them, and often lamented the unchristian spirit of those who denied that the Baptist churches were churches at all, and otherwise scornfully assailed brethren with whom they were agreed in all other matters. He had no cause to shrink from combat on his own account, for he was so able a polemic that sometimes the mere outline of his argument sufficed to let his opponents see that they had no very desirable task before them. An amusing instance of this is recorded by Crosby in the following paragraph: –

"He was challenged by some ministers of the Church of England, not far from London, to dispute on baptism; and the place appointed was at Gravesend. As he was going thither in a Gravesend boat, in company with others, there happened to be a clergyman in the same boat with him. The conversation Mr Keach had in the boat, with some of his friends, caused this clergyman to suspect he was the person going to dispute with his brethren, and accordingly he attacked him in the boat, and from hence saw the defence he was able to make, and what little credit would be obtained on their side of the question. As soon as the boat arrived at Gravesend this clergyman hastened to his friends, and let them know the conversation he had had with Mr Keach in the boat, and what arguments he intended to urge; which put an entire stop to the disputation, and Mr Keach returned to London again without seeing any one of them. Though they had rendered the Baptists as contemptible as they could by stating that they had nothing to say for their practice in baptising adult persons, yet when all came to all, not one of them dared to appear and defend what they had spoken."

Another method of usefulness very largely used by Mr Keach was the publication of books. He is the author of two well-known folios, "*Key to open Scripture Metaphors,*" and an "*Exposition of the Parables.*" These works have long enjoyed a high repute, and though they are now regarded as out of date, the time was when they were so universally used by ministers, the "Key to the Metaphors" especially, that Dr Adam Clarke complains of the too great dependence of preachers upon them. Keach wrote in all forty-three works – eighteen practical, sixteen polemical, and nine poetical. These books were mostly embellished with curious wood-engravings and were sold as chap-books by hawkers from town to town. Some of these such as "*War with the Devil*" and "*Travels of True Godliness*" must have been very popular, for we have seen the 22nd editions, and there were probably more. Those issued by Keach himself have most reputable engravings, in the best style of art of those days, of which we have

given two specimens from one of his own editions, but editions subsequent to his death are produced in the very worst manner, and like Hodge's razors, were evidently only meant "to sell." Our copy of the wood block, of "London in flames," is rather a favourable specimen of these wretched productions.

As for the poetry of Keach's works, the less said the better. It is a rigmarole almost equal to John Bunyan's rhyming, but hardly up even to the mark of honest John. We will inflict none of it upon our readers, except a few lines from his "*War with the Devil*": –

"I never read of *Peter's* triple crown,
  Nor that he ever wore a Popish gown;
  I never learn'd that he did Pope become,
  Or rul'd o'er kings, like to the beasts of *Rome*,
  I never learn'd he granted dispensations,
  To poison kings or rulers of those nations
  Who were profane, or turned heretics,
  Or did refuse the faith of Catholics.
  I read not that he's called His Holiness,
  Yet he'd as much as any Pope, I guess;
  I never learn'd *Peter* did magnify
  Himself above all gods, or God on high!
  Or that upon the necks of kings he trod,
  Or ever he in cloth of gold was clad;
  I never read that he made laws to burn
  Such as were heretics, and would not turn
  To Jesus Christ, much less to murder those
  Who did, in truth, idolatry oppose.
  I never learn'd, nor could do, to this day,
  That Pope and *Peter* walk'd both in one way;
  Yea, or that they in anything accord,
  Save only in denying of the Lord:
  Peter deny'd him, yet did love him dear;
  The Pope denies him, and doth hatred bear
  To him, and to all those that do him love,
  Who bear his image and are from above.
  Peter deny'd him, and did weep amain,
  The Pope denies him but with great disdain.
  Peter deny'd him, yet for him did die,
  The Pope in malice doth him crucify.
  Peter deny'd him thrice, and then repented,
  The Pope a thousand times, but ne'er relented."

Very sweetly did Mr Keach preach the great fundamental truths of the gospel, and glorify the name and work of Jesus. His *"Gospel Mine Opened,"* and other works, rich in savour, show that he was no mere stickler for a point of ceremony, but one who loved the whole truth as it is in Jesus, and felt its power. The doctrine of the Second Advent evidently had great charms for him, but not so as to crowd out Christ crucified. He was very solid in his preaching, and his whole conduct and behaviour betokened a man deeply in earnest for the cause of God. In addressing the ungodly he was intensely direct, solemn, and impressive, not flinching to declare the terrors of the Lord, nor veiling the freeness of divine grace. We quote a few sentences from one of his sermons, only remarking that such clear evangelical statements are found throughout all his works. "We preach to you, sinners, that Jesus Christ will entertain you, if you come to him, bid you welcome, and not cast you off because of the greatness of your sins, though you have no qualifications to recommend you to him. Would you wash yourselves from your sins, and then come to the fountain of his blood to be washed? We hold forth Christ to be your whole Saviour, and that he is 'set forth as the propitiation through faith in his blood;' whom if you close with, and believe in, you shall be justified: we tell you God justifies the ungodly, – they that are so before being justified ... Therefore, sinners, though 'tis your duty to reform your lives, and leave your abominable sins, which often bring heavy judgments upon you in this world, and expose you to eternal wrath in the world to come; yet know that all that you can do will fail in point of your acceptance and justification in God's sight, or to save your souls; your present work and business is to believe in Jesus Christ, to look to him, who alone can renew his sacred image in your souls, and make you new creatures, which must be done, or you perish. O cry that he would help your unbelief. Come, venture your souls on Christ's righteousness; Christ is able to save you though you are ever so great sinners. Come to him, throw yourselves at the feet of Jesus. *Look to Jesus*, who came to seek and save them that were lost. 'If any man thirst, let him come unto me, and drink,' *John 7:37, 38*. You may have the water of life freely. Do not say, 'I want qualifications or a meetness to come to Christ.' Sinner, dost thou thirst? Dost thou see a want of righteousness? 'Tis not a righteousness; but 'tis a sense of the want of righteousness, which is rather the qualification thou shouldst look at. Christ hath righteousness sufficient to clothe you, bread of life to feed you, grace to adorn you. Whatever you want, it is to be had in him. We tell you there is help in him, salvation in him. 'Through the propitiation in his blood' you must be justified, and that by faith alone."

For the interests of his denomination Keach was a zealous and judicious worker: he was one of the most earnest in inducing the Baptist churches to give a suitable maintenance to their ministers which, partly from poverty and persecution, and partly also from mistaken notions, they had very generally neglected to do. At an assembly of a hundred churches which met in London, his little book, "*The Minister's Maintenance Vindicated*," was ordered to be dispersed among the congregations. Mr Keach was also very greatly the means of leading back the Baptists to the habit of congregational singing. Because from fear of discovery by the magistrates the assemblies of believers had been unable to sing, the habit of songless worship had been acquired in many congregations, and when happier days gave opportunity for praising the Lord with the voice, the older folks looked upon it as an innovation, and would have none of it. "When he was convinced that singing the praises of God was a holy ordinance of Jesus Christ, he laboured earnestly and with a great deal of prudence to convince his people thereof; and first obtained their consent to the practice of it at the conclusion of the Lord's Supper, and had but two of the brethren in the church who opposed him therein. (These two seem to have made great complaint of the fact 'that many of the honest hearers, who stayed to see the supper, sung with them.' A terrible calamity certainly.) After the church had continued in this practice about six years, they further consented to practise the same on public thanksgiving days, and continued therein about fourteen years. Even this, however, does not seem to have been continuously carried out, and the grumbling few complained that on one occasion, 'when the minister had ended his exercise, a hymn was given up to him, by whom we know not (except it were by Mr Keach's means), which he read and sang and the people with him; but this was not in the least by the appointment of the church, but an imposition on them.' In due time by a regular act of the church, it was agreed to sing the praises of God on every Lord's Day. There were only about five or six persons that dissented therefrom, but so far was Mr Keach, or the church, from imposing on the consciences of those few that dissented (though the church then consisted of some hundreds) that they agreed to sing when prayer was concluded after the sermon, and if those few who were not satisfied could not stay the time of singing, they might freely go out, and the church would not be offended at them. Notwithstanding the care and consideration, however, the malcontents would not yield. They withdrew, and founded another church upon the same principles, *singing only excepted*, so difficult was it to remove longstanding prejudices." The secession formed that right worthy and well-beloved church which has for many years continued to meet in the chapel in Maze Pond, until now it seeks another local habitation in the Old Kent Road. It was some time before the Maze Pond friends learned to sing, but it is needless to say that in due time they became as fond of making melody unto the Lord as the brethren from whom they parted. There can be no doubt that the separation strengthened the denomination by giving it two earnest churches instead of one, and therefore we conclude that, however strange the immediate cause, it was of the Lord. The two churches have lived on the happiest terms, and have again and again accommodated each other, when either meeting-house has been under repair. Happily this was the only division which vexed the fellowship under Mr Keach, though the Quakers at one time, and the seventh-day Baptists at another, caused some trouble and discussion. The pastor was a power in the church, and by the weight of his mind and character directed it aright, so that troublers found it expedient to carry out their mission in some less consolidated community. He could also wax warm, and deliver his mind with vehemence, and then it was somewhat dangerous to be his opponent. Mr Keach was not, however, apt to spend his time in contention. He was a practical man, and trained his church to labour in the service of the Lord. Several were by his means called into the Christian ministry, his own son, Elias Keach, among them. He was mighty at home and useful abroad. By his means other churches were founded and meeting-houses erected; he was in fact as a pillar and a brazen wall among the Baptist churches of his day, and was in consequence deservedly had in honour. We find his name among others convening the first assembly of Particular Baptists, and as agreeing to the confession of faith which was issued by that body. His name also appears at the foot of calls to public fasts and thanksgivings, which were held by the denomination. He was a leading spirit in the Baptist body.

"Mr Keach was of a very weak constitution, being often afflicted with illness, and once to such a degree that he was given over by the physicians; and several of the ministers, and his relations, had taken their leave of him as a dying man and past all hope of recovery; but the Rev Mr Hanserd Knollys, seeing his friend and brother in the gospel so near expiring, betook himself to prayer, and in a very extraordinary manner begged that God would spare him, and add unto his days the time he granted to his servant Hezekiah. As soon as he had ended his prayer, he said, 'Brother Keach, I shall be in heaven before you,' and quickly after left him. So remarkable was the answer of God to this good man's prayer, that we cannot omit it; though it may be discredited by some, there were many who could bear incontestable testimony to the fact. Mr Keach recovered of that illness, and lived just fifteen years afterwards; and then it pleased God to visit him with that short sickness which put an end to his days." He "fell on sleep" July 16th, 1704, in the sixty-fourth year of his age, and was buried at the Baptists' burying ground *in the Park, Southwark.* It was not a little singular that in after years the church over which he so ably presided should pitch its tent so near the place where his bones were laid, and New Park Street should appear in her annals as a well-beloved name.

Here perhaps is the fittest place to insert "The Solemn Covenant," to which all the members of the church subscribed in the days of Mr Keach. It must commend itself to the judgement of all candid Christians. Would to God that all our churches were mindful of the sacred relationship which exists among Christians, and attended to the duties arising out of it.

The Solemn Covenant of the Church at its Constitution

We who desire to walk together in the fear of the Lord, do, through the assistance of his Holy Spirit, profess our deep and serious humiliation for all our transgressions. And we do solemnly, in the presence of God, of each other, in the sense of our own unworthiness, give up ourselves to the Lord, in a church state according to the apostolical constitution, that he may be our God, and we may be his people, through the everlasting covenant of his free grace, in which alone we hope to be accepted by him, through his blessed Son Jesus Christ, whom we take to be our High Priest, to justify and sanctify us, and our Prophet to teach us; and to be subject to him as our Law-giver, and the King of Saints; and to conform to all his holy laws and ordinances, for our growth, establishment, and consolation; that we may be as a holy spouse unto him, and serve him in our generation, and wait for his second appearance, as our glorious Bridegroom.

Being fully satisfied in the way of church communion, and the truth of grace in some good measure upon one another's spirits, we do solemnly join ourselves together in a holy union and fellowship, humbly submitting to the discipline of the gospel, and all holy duties required of a people in such a spiritual relation.

1. We do promise and engage to walk in all holiness, godliness, humility, and brotherly love, as much as in us lieth to render our communion delightful to God, comfortable to ourselves, and lovely to the rest of the Lord's people.

2. We do promise to watch over each other's conversations, and not to suffer sin upon one another, so far as God shall discover it to us, or any of us; and to stir up one another to love and good works; to warn, rebuke, and admonish one another with meekness, according to the rules left to us of Christ in that behalf.

3. We do promise in an especial manner to pray for one another, and for the glory and increase of this church, and for the presence of God in it, and the pouring forth of his Spirit on it, and his protection over it to his glory.

4. We do promise to bear one another's burdens, to cleave to one another, and to have a fellow-feeling with one another, in all conditions both outward and inward, as God in his providence shall cast any of us into.

5. We do promise to bear with one another's weaknesses, failings, and infirmities, with much tenderness, not discovering them to any without the Church, nor any within, unless according to Christ's rule, and the order of the gospel provided in that case.

6. We do promise to strive together for the truth of the gospel and purity of God's ways and ordinances, to avoid causes, and causers of division, endeavouring to keep the unity of the Spirit in the bond of peace. *Ephesians 4:3.*

7. We do promise to meet together on Lord's Days, and at other times, as the Lord shall give us opportunities, to serve and glorify God in the way of his worship, to edify one another, and to contrive the good of his church.

8. We do promise according to our ability (or as God shall bless us with the good things of this world) to communicate to our pastor or minister, God having ordained that they that preach the gospel should live of the gospel. (And now can anything lay a greater obligation upon the conscience than this covenant, what then is the sin of such who violate it?)

These and all other gospel duties we humbly submit unto, promising and purposing to perform, not in our own strength, being conscious of our own weakness, but in the power and strength of the blessed God, whose we are, and whom we desire to serve. To whom be glory now and for evermore. Amen.

3
Benjamin Stinton

When Mr Keach was upon his death-bed he sent for his son-in-law, BENJAMIN STINTON, and solemnly charged him to care for the church which he was about to leave, and especially urged him to accept the pastoral office should it be offered to him by the brethren. Mr Stinton had already for some years helped his father-in-law in many ways, and therefore he was no new and untried man. It is no small blessing when a church can find her pastors in her own midst; the rule is to look abroad, but perhaps if our home gifts were more encouraged the Holy Spirit would cause our teachers to come forth more frequently from among our own brethren. Still we cannot forget the proverb about a prophet in his own country. When the church gave Mr Stinton a pressing invitation, he delayed a while, and gave himself space for serious consideration; but at length remembering the dying words of his father-in-law, and feeling himself directed by the Spirit of God, he gave himself up to the ministry, which he faithfully discharged for 14 years – namely, from 1704 to 1718.

Mr Stinton had great natural gifts, but felt in need of more education, and set himself to work to obtain it as soon as he was settled over the church. Thoroughly to be furnished for the great work before him was his first endeavour. Crosby says of him: "He was a very painful and laborious minister of the gospel, and though he had not the advantage of an academical education, yet by his own industry, under the assistance of the famous Mr Ainsworth (author of the Latin dictionary), after he had taken upon him the ministerial office, he acquired a good degree of knowledge in the languages, and other useful parts of literature, which added lustre to those natural endowments which were very conspicuous in him."

He will be best remembered for the zealous part which he took in movements for the general good. He was the originator with others of the Protestant Dissenters' Charity School in Horselydown, at which conscientious dissenters were able to obtain an education for their children without their being compelled to attend the Established Church and learn the Catechism. To assist in the maintenance of this school, an evening lecture was established on the Lord's Day at Mr Stinton's meeting-house, at which six ministers officiated in turns.

We find that Mr Stinton and his church organised efforts to repair and rebuild a Common Baptistery in Horselydown, to which the various churches were able to bring their candidates for baptism, and administer the ordinance comfortably and decorously. Very few meeting-houses at that time possessed baptisteries of their own, and as these places were usually small it was not easy to provide proper vestries and robing-rooms. At the Common Baptistery every convenience could be provided for all the churches which chose to use it.

But the grand achievement of this pastorate was the establishment of THE BAPTIST FUND. Mr Stinton was one of the chief originators if not the first mover in the establishment of this fund, which has been the means of untold benefit to the Baptist denomination. Its first object is to make due provision for the honourable maintenance of poor ministers, and to assist in training up others to succeed them in their office. How great a need there was in the matter of ministerial poverty is too clear from a resolution of the managers of the fund that none were eligible to receive assistance who received more than £25 per annum from their congregations. What true devotion must have fired the breasts of men who could bear such penury for Christ's sake! It was time that such extreme poverty should not be allowed to exist needlessly, and that sufferers should be generously assisted. To this end certain churches subscribed a capital sum to form the basis of the fund: Mr Stinton's church giving £150, and being therefore entitled to send the pastor and three delegates to vote upon the distribution of the moneys. The fund has now a large sum to expend annually, and thereby helps struggling pastors, gives grants of books to students, and spends an amount annually upon the education of young men for the ministry. The fund is called THE PARTICULAR BAPTIST FUND, as being intended to aid Calvinistic rather than Arminian Baptists. This was not at all to the mind of Stinton, who desired to have the fund established for the benefit of all Baptists who held the great fundamentals of the gospel. Although himself a Calvinistic Baptist, he thought it unlovely to divide the body with a hard and fast line, and unwise to open doors for constant dispute and disunion. Finding that his views were not endorsed by the other brethren, he entered his protest, and then proceeded to aid them to the utmost of his power in their more limited design. He was not impractical, and in this he far surpassed certain pretentious Liberals of the present day, who will do nothing if they may not attempt everything.

In the later days of Mr Stinton, as the lease of the meeting-house in Goat's Yard was nearly run out, preparation was made for erecting a new place of worship in Unicorn Yard.

Spending himself in various works of usefulness, Mr Stinton worked on until the 11th of February, 1718, when a sudden close was put to his labours and his life. He was taken suddenly ill, and saying to his wife, "*I am going,*" he laid himself down upon the bed, and expired in the forty-third year of his life. He smiled on death, for the Lord smiled on him. He was buried near his predecessor, in the Park, Southwark.

4
John Gill

THE loss of its pastor is always a serious matter to a Baptist church, not only because it is deprived of the services of a well-tried and faithful guide, but because in the process of selecting a successor some of the worst points of human nature are too apt to come to the front. All may unite in the former pastor, but where will they find another rallying point? So many men, so many minds. All are not prepared to forego their own predilections, some are ready to be litigious, and a few seize the opportunity to thrust themselves into undue prominence. If they would all wait upon the Lord for his guidance, and consent to follow it when they have obtained it, the matter would move smoothly; but, alas, it is not always so. In the present instance there came before the church an excellent young man, whose later life proved that he was well qualified for the pastorate, but either he was too young, being only twenty or twenty-one years of age, or there were certain points in his manner which were not pleasing to the older friends, and therefore he was earnestly opposed. The deacons, with the exception of Mr Thomas Crosby, schoolmaster, and son-in-law of Keach, were resolved that this young man, who was none other than JOHN GILL from Kettering, should not become the pastor. He found, however, warm and numerous supporters, and when the question came to a vote, his admirers claimed the majority, and in all probability their claim was correct, for the other party declined a scrutiny of the votes, and also raised the question of the women's voting, declaring, what was no doubt true, that apart from the female vote John Gill was in the minority. The end of the difference was that about half the church withdrew from the chapel in Goat Yard, and met in Mr Crosby's schoolroom, claiming to be the old church, while

John Gill

another portion remained in the chapel, and also maintained that they were the original church. The question is now of small consequence, if it ever had any importance, for the company who rejected Gill, after selecting an excellent preacher, and prospering for many years, met with a chequered experience, and at length ceased to exist. In all probability the division promoted the growth of the cause of Christ, and whatever unhappy circumstances marred it for a while, both parties acted conscientiously, and in a very short time were perfectly reconciled to each other. Mr Gill's people did not long worship in Crosby's schoolroom, but as the other friends were moving out and erecting another meeting-house in Unicorn Yard, they came back to the old building in Goat Yard, and found themselves very much at home. Crosby, however, quarrelled with the pastor and left him, and with some others of his own family went to the other community in Unicorn Yard. We suspect that Mr Gill had preached a little too dogmatically for the schoolmaster, and proved himself to be a more thorough-going Calvinist, and a more rigid doctrinalist than the brother-in-law of Stinton quite approved. It was not very surprising that he should turn against the man of his choice, for it has happened times without number, that men who are warm partisans are apt to become fierce opponents when their man does not prove to be subservient, and will not be moulded at their will. The friend is apt to assume the airs of a patron, and talk about ingratitude, but with men like John Gill this would never succeed.

As Dr Gill's ministry extended over no less a period than fifty-one years, reaching from 1720 to 1771, and as he proved himself to be a true master in Israel, we shall need more than the usual space in which to describe him. His entire ministry was crowned with more than ordinary success, and he was by far the greatest scholar the church had yet chosen, but he cannot be regarded as so great a soul-winner as Keach had been, neither was the church at any time so numerous under his ministry as under that of Keach. His method of address to sinners, in which for many years a large class of preachers followed him, was not likely to be largely useful. He cramped himself, and was therefore straitened where there was no scriptural reason for being so. He does not appear to have had the public spirit of Stinton, though he had a far larger share of influence in the churches, and was indeed a sort of archbishop over a certain section. The ordination discourses and funeral sermons which he preached must have amounted to a very large number: it seemed as if no Particular Baptist minister could be properly inducted or interred without Dr Gill's officiating. We shall, however, be more likely to give our readers an idea of this truly great man if we set forth such details of his life as we can gather.

John Gill was born at Kettering, in Northamptonshire, November 23, 1697. His father, Edward Gill, first became a member of the Dissenting congregation in that place, consisting then of Presbyterians, Independents, and Baptists. Besides their pastor, they had a teaching elder of the Baptist denomination, Mr William Wallis, who was the administrator of baptism, by immersion, to such persons among them as desired it; but at length the baptised believers having been rendered uncomfortable in their communion, by some particular persons, they were obliged to separate, with Mr William Wallis, their teacher, and formed themselves into a distinct church of the *Particular Baptist* denomination. Among the number was Mr Edward Gill, who in due time was chosen to the office of deacon among them.

Young John Gill, with the dawn of reason, discovered a fine capacity for learning; and, being soon out of the reach of common teachers, he was very early sent to the grammar school in the town, which he attended with uncommon diligence and unwearied application, quickly surpassing those of his own age, and others who were considerably his seniors. Here he continued until he was eleven years old. During this time, notwithstanding the tedious manner in which grammatical knowledge was then conveyed, besides going through the common school books, he mastered the principal Latin classics, and made such a proficiency in the Greek as obtained for him marks of distinction from several of the neighbouring clergy, who were good enough occasionally to examine and encourage his progress, when they met him at a bookseller's shop in the town, which he constantly attended on market days, the only time it was open. Here he so regularly attended, for the sake of consulting different authors, that it became the usual asseveration with the people of the neighbourhood, when speaking of anything they considered certain – "it is as sure," said they, "as that John Gill is in the bookseller's shop." And as the same studious disposition attended him through life, so did nearly the same remark: those who knew usually employing this mode of affirmation, "as surely as Dr Gill is in his study."

As the precocious talents of young Gill were also attended with early piety, he was baptised and received into the church in Kettering in his nineteenth year, and, at the request of the church, very soon began to preach among them. This led to his removing to Higham Ferrers, a small borough town in Northamptonshire, where he lived near a minister of learning who helped him in his studies. His name appears at this time upon the books of the Baptist Fund as receiving £16 during his twentieth and twenty-first years. Little did the church in Goat's Yard know when it subscribed to the fund, that one of its future eminent pastors would be an early recipient of its bounty. At Higham Ferrers Gill married, but did not long continue in the place, returning to reside in Kettering.

A lady who was present when John Gill preached his very *first* sermon at Kettering, also heard him deliver his *last* in London, more than fifty years later. *After* his death she joined the church over which he had presided, relating at some length a truly interesting experience, which gave universal pleasure to all who heard it. Her name was Mary Bailey, and it is to be hoped that none will imitate her by postponing the confession of their faith in Jesus for so long a time. She lived half a century in disobedience to her Lord, and even when she avowed his name, it must have caused her deep regret that she had lingered so long in neglect of the Redeemer's ordinance.

In the beginning of the year 1719, the church at Horsleydown invited him to preach with a view to the pastorate. As we have already seen, there was a determined opposition to him in about one half of the church. The matter was referred to the club of ministers meeting at the Hanover Coffee house, and they gave the absurd advice that the two parties should each hear their own man turn about till they could agree. Common sense came to the rescue, and this sort of religious duel never came off. The friends with far greater wisdom divided. John Gill's friends secured the old meeting-house for the term of forty years, and he was ordained March 22, 1720.

Little did the friends dream what sort of man they had thus chosen to be their teacher; but had they known it, they would have rejoiced that a man of such vast erudition, such indefatigable industry, such sound judgement, and such sterling honesty, had come among them. He was to be more mighty with his pen than Keach, and to make a deeper impression upon his age, though perhaps with the tongue he was less powerful than his eminent predecessor. Early in his ministry he had to take up the cudgels for Baptist views against a Paedobaptist preacher of Rowel, near Kettering, and he did so in a manner worthy of that eulogium which Toplady passed upon him in reference to other controversies, when he compared him to Marlborough, and declared that he never fought a battle without winning it.

Mr Gill, being settled in London, became more intimately acquainted with that worthy minister of the gospel, Mr John Skepp, pastor of the Baptist church at Cripplegate. This gentleman, though he had not a liberal education, yet, after he came into the ministry, through great diligence acquired a large acquaintance with the Hebrew tongue. As Mr Gill had previously taken great delight in the Hebrew, his conversation with this worthy minister rekindled a flame of fervent desire to obtain a more extensive knowledge of it, and especially of Rabbinical learning. Mr Skepp dying a year or two after, Mr Gill purchased most of his Hebrew works, the Baptist Fund making him a grant of £17 10s. for this purpose. Having obtained the books, he went to work with great eagerness, reading the Targums and ancient commentaries, and in a course of between twenty and thirty years' acquaintance with these writings he collected a large number of learned observations. Having also, in this time, gone through certain books of the *Old Testament* and almost the whole of the *New Testament*, by way of *Exposition*, in the course of his ministry, he put all the expository, critical, and illustrative parts together, and in the year 1745 issued proposals for publishing his *"Exposition of the whole New Testament,"* in three volumes folio. The work meeting due encouragement, it was put to press the same year, and was finished, the first volume in 1746, the second in 1747, and the third in 1748. Towards the close of the publication of this work, in 1748, Mr Gill received a diploma from Marischal College,

Aberdeen, creating him Doctor in Divinity on account of his knowledge of the Scriptures, of the Oriental languages and of Jewish antiquities. When his deacons in London congratulated him on the respect which had been shown him, he thanked them, pleasantly adding, *I neither thought it, nor bought it, nor sought it.*

The ministry of Mr Gill being acceptable not only to his own people but to many persons of different denominations, several gentlemen proposed among themselves to set up a week-day lecture, that they might have an opportunity of hearing him. Accordingly they formed themselves into a society, and agreed to have a lecture on Wednesday evenings, in Great Eastcheap, and set on foot a subscription to support it. Upon their invitation Mr Gill undertook the lectureship. He opened it in the year 1729, with a discourse or two on *Psalm 71:16:* "I will go in the strength of the Lord God: I will make mention of thy righteousness, even of thine only." Through divine grace he was enabled to abide by this resolution to the edification of many, preaching in Great Eastcheap for more than twenty-six years, and only relinquished the lecture when the infirmities of years were telling upon him, and he felt a great desire to give all his time to the completion of his great expository works.

If it be enquired how he distributed his time, and whether he indulged himself in any relaxation, we are able to reply. When the doctor was asked by Mr Ryland how it was that he had performed such vast labours, he answered, it was not done by very early rising, nor by sitting up late – the latter he was confident must be injurious to any student, and not helpful. The truth is, he rose as soon as it was light in the winter, and usually before six in the summer, in the last part of his life not quite so early. He breakfasted constantly in his study, and always on chocolate, but came down with his family to dinner, and carved for them. Through the latter years of his life he seldom went into his study after tea, unless about an hour in summer, but sat below reading some book, or correcting his sheets as they were issuing from the press, and with some of these he had care enough, partly caused by his own indistinct handwriting, for toward the end of his life he wrote very small and illegibly, and partly by the inattention or incompetency of the compositors, from whom we are certain he has been under the necessity of getting six or seven revisions of a sheet, especially of such sheets as contained learned quotations. (Alas! in all ages, compositors and authors have been a mutual plague! We have no doubt that in Gill's case the workmen were more sinned against than sinning: if his writing was small and illegible, who wonders that compositors blundered?)

He was never distinguished for the length or frequency of his pastoral visits, and in this he is not an example. Yet probably his time was more profitable to the church of God in the study than it could have been had he spent it in going from door to door.

It was his practice, once a week, to meet his ministering brethren at the accustomed coffee house, where a sort of ministers' club assembled, or else to spend a friendly hour with them under the hospitable roof of Thomas Watson, an honoured member of the Baptist church then meeting near Cripplegate. That gentleman kept an open table on Tuesdays for the dissenting ministers of the three denominations. The doctor generally met with them, took his part cheerfully in conversation, and maintained it on their return home, whether they came back on foot or by the boat.

As a pastor he presided over the flock with dignity and affection. In the course of his ministry he had some weak, some unworthy, and some very wicked persons to deal with. To the feeble of the flock he was an affectionate friend and father. He readily bore with their weaknesses, failings, and infirmities, and particularly when he saw they were sincerely on the Lord's side. A godly woman visited him one day, in great trouble, about the singing; for the clerk, in about three years, had introduced two new tunes. Not that he was a famous singer, or able to conduct a great variety of song, but he did his best. The young people were pleased with the new tunes; but the good woman could not bear the innovation. The Doctor, after patiently listening, asked her whether she understood singing? No, she said. "What! Can't you sing?" No, she was no singer, nor her aged father before her. And though they had had about a hundred years between them to learn the Old Hundredth tune, they could not sing it, *nor any other tune.* The doctor did not hurt her feelings by telling her that people who did not understand singing were the last who should complain; but he meekly said, "Sister, what tunes should you like us to sing?" "Why, Sir," she replied, "I should very much like David's tunes." "Well," said he, "if you will get David's tunes for us, we can then try to sing them." Such weak good people may be found among all denominations of Christians.

Dr Gill was sometimes accosted by rude people, even in his own congregation. A cynical old man, who we would charitably hope was a little touched in the head, had taken an antipathy against some of his minister's tenets, more than once had grinned contempt at him from the gallery. Then he tried another method of annoyance, and would meet him at the foot of the pulpit-stairs, and ask, "Is this preaching?" repeating his question, "Is this preaching?" The insolence at first met with no answer from the preacher, but, it seems, he determined not to be often treated in this manner. Not long after, the said churl, planting himself again in the same position, expressed his contempt somewhat louder. "Is this the great Doctor Gill?" The Doctor, immediately, addressed him with the full strength of his voice, and looking him in the face, and pointing him to the pulpit, said, "*Go up and do better – go up and do better.*" This was answering a fool according to his folly; and the reply afforded gratification to all who heard it.

All the stories told of Dr Gill are somewhat grim. He could not come down to the level of men and women of the common order so far as to be jocose, and when he attempted to do so, he looked like Hercules with the distaff, or Goliath threading a needle. When he verged upon the humorous the jokes were ponderous and overwhelming, burying his adversary as well as crushing him. It is said that a garrulous dame once called upon him to find fault with the excessive length of his white bands. "Well, well," said the doctor, "what do you think is the right length? Take them and make them as long or as short as you like." The lady expressed her delight; she was sure that her dear pastor would grant her request, and therefore she had brought her scissors with her and would do the trimming at once. Accordingly snip, snip, and the thing was done and the bibs returned. "Now," said the Doctor, "my good sister, you must do me a good turn also." "Yes, that I will, Doctor. What can it be?" "Well – you have something about you which is a deal too long, and causes me no end of trouble, and I should like to see it shorter." "Indeed, dear sir, I will not hesitate," said the dame, "what is it, here are the scissors, use them as you please." "Come then," said the pastor, "*good sister, put out your tongue.*" We have often pictured him sitting in the old chair which is preserved in our vestry, and thus quietly rebuking the gossip.

Dr Gill's chair

The comparative asperity of his manner was probably the result of his secluded habits and also of that sturdy firmness of mind which in other directions revealed itself so admirably. When he was once warned that the publication of a certain book would lose him many supporters and reduce his income, he did not hesitate for a moment, but replied, *"Do not tell me of losing. I value nothing in comparison with Gospel truth. I am not afraid to be poor."*

He had, however, a warm heart beneath his stern exterior, and was full of tenderness, especially in the domestic circle. We read that he went down to Kettering every year to spend a few days with his mother, so long as she lived, and when the news of her death reached him he laid down his pipe and never smoked again. His old country friends were always welcome at his house, and in their society he would seem to have unbent far more than one would have expected. With Mr Clayton, of Steventon, and other plain men, he would be much at home, and they made very free with him. When this friend once came to London the doctor said, "Brother Clayton, what have you been about? They tell me that you have been expounding *Revelation*. A man who enters upon that work should first have some acquaintance with history, the prophecies in general, and many other things!" "Why, doctor," said Mr Clayton, "I did as well as I could, and you can't do any better." Such simplicity tickled the doctor amazingly, and it was commonly said that he laughed more heartily that part of the year when Mr Clayton was in town than he did all the year besides.

In the year 1752 Dr Gill had a very memorable escape from being killed in his study. On March the 15th, in the morning, there was a violent hurricane, which much damaged many houses both in London and Westminster. Soon after he had left his study, to go to preach, a stack of chimneys fell through the roof into his study, breaking his writing table to pieces, and must have killed him had the fall happened a little sooner. Seriously noticing this remarkable preservation to a friend who had some time before repeated a saying of Dr Halley, the great astronomer, "That great study prolonged a man's life, by keeping him out of harm's way;" he said, *"What becomes of Dr Halley's words now, since a man may come to danger and harm in his own closet, as well as on the highway, if not protected by the special care of God's providence?"*

In 1757, the church under his care erected a new meeting-house for him in Carter Lane, St Olave's Street, near London Bridge, Southwark; which he opened October 9, preaching two sermons on *Exodus 20:24*. These he afterwards printed, entitling them "Attendance in places of religious worship, where the Divine name is recorded, encouraged." In one of these discourses is this paragraph: "As we have now opened a new place of worship, we enter upon it, recording the name of the Lord, by preaching the doctrines of the grace of God, and of free and full salvation by Jesus Christ; and by the administration of gospel ordinances, as they have been delivered to us. What doctrines may be taught in this place, after I am gone, is not for me to know; but, as for my own part, I am at a point; I am determined, and have been long ago, what to make the subject of my ministry. It is now upwards of forty years since I entered into the arduous work, and the first sermon I ever preached was from those words of the apostle: '*For I am determined not to know anything among you, save Jesus Christ, and him crucified.*' Through the grace of God, I have been enabled, in some good measure, to abide by the same resolution hitherto, as many of you here are my witnesses; and I hope, through Divine assistance, I ever shall, as long as I am in this tabernacle, and engaged in such a work. *I am not afraid of the reproaches of men; I have been* INURED TO THESE, FROM MY YOUTH UPWARDS; *none of these things move me.*"

Our view of Carter Lane Chapel will not fascinate the reader; we have had to take it from a model in the possession of a former member of the church. We trust the building was not so ugly as our drawing.

Carter Lane Chapel

In the Doctor's later years the congregations were sparse and the membership seriously declined. He was himself only able to preach once on the Sabbath, and living in a rural retreat in Camberwell, he could do but little in the way of overseeing the church. It was thought desirable that some younger minister should be found to act as co-pastor. To this the Doctor gave a very decided answer in the negative, asserting "that Christ gives pastors is certain, but that he gives *co-pastors* is not so certain." He even went as far as comparing a church with a co-pastor to a woman who should marry another man while her first husband lived, and call him a co-husband. In view of the many disagreements and unhappinesses resulting from co-pastorships, we feel half inclined to admire the Doctor's refusal; and remembering what sort of man he was, we question if a co-pastor would have worked happily with him, but his arguments against the proposition were preposterous, and in our own instance, in the self-same church, two brothers have worked together for years with the utmost harmony, and nothing has occurred to make us fear that the position of affairs is displeasing to the great Head of the church. Great men are not always wise. However, by his stern repudiation of any division of his authority the old gentleman held the reins of power until the age of seventy-four, although the young people gradually dropped off and the church barely numbered 150 members.

The intense admiration and love of his flock is proved by the letter sent to him in reply to his refusal to have an assistant. They defer at once to this judgment, and declare that they never wished to do more than consult him with the utmost deference, and then they conclude by saying, "We greatly fear that you apprehend an abatement in our affection toward you. *That we are not conscious of,* we think it impossible that our love should be easily removed from him who has instrumentally been made so useful to our souls; but we trust our hearts are knit as the heart of one man toward you, as the servant of Christ, and as our father in the Gospel of our Lord Jesus. Another grieving circumstance is, that if the church is willing, you seem inclined to resign your office as pastor. This expression is extremely alarming to us, and is what can by no means find a place in our thoughts, it being our fixed desire and continual prayer, that you may live and die in that endeared relation. We say with united voice, How can a father give up his children, or affectionate children their father? Dear Sir, we beseech you not to cast us off, but bear us upon your heart and spiritual affections all your days, and let us be remembered to God through your prayers, and who knows but the Lord may visit us again and make us to break forth on the right hand and on the left?" This was signed by all the brethren.

In a few weeks the venerable divine became too feeble for pulpit service and confined himself to his study and the writing-desk, and by-and-bye found that he must lie down to rest, for his day's work was done. He died as he had lived, in a calm, quiet manner, resting on that rich sovereign grace which it had been his joy to preach. To his dear relative, the Rev John Gill, of St Albans, he thus expressed himself: "I depend wholly and alone upon the free, sovereign, eternal, unchangeable, love of God, the firm and everlasting covenant of grace, and my interest in the persons of the Trinity, for my whole salvation; and not upon any righteousness of my own; nor upon anything done in me, or done by me, under the influences of the Holy Spirit."

Nearly in the same words he expressed himself to others. To one he said, "I have nothing to make me uneasy," and then repeated the following lines from Dr Watts, in honour of the adored Redeemer: —

> "He raised me from the deeps of sin,
>   The gates of gaping hell,
> And fix'd my standing more secure,
>   Than 'twas before I fell."

The last words he was heard to speak were, "O my Father, my Father!" He died at Camberwell, October 14, 1771, and was buried in Bunhill Fields. His eyesight had been preserved to him so that he could read small print by candlelight even to the last, and he never used glasses. His was a mind and frame of singular vigour, and he died before failing sight, either mental or physical, rendered him unfit for service: in this as highly favoured as he had been in most other respects. He was one of the most learned men that the Baptist denomination has ever produced. His great work, "*The Exposition of the Old and New Testament*," is still held in the highest esteem even by those whose sentiments differ widely from the author's. His "*Body of Divinity*" is also a masterly condensation of doctrinal and practical theology, and his "*Cause of God and Truth*" is highly esteemed by many. The system of theology with which many identify his name has chilled many churches to their very soul, for it has led them to omit the free invitations of the gospel, and to deny that it is the duty of sinners to believe in Jesus: but for this Dr Gill must not be altogether held responsible, for a candid reader of his commentary will soon perceive in it expressions altogether out of accord with such a narrow system; and it is well known that when he was dealing with practical godliness he was so bold in his utterances that the devotees of Hyper-Calvinism could not endure him. "Well, Sir," said one of these, "if I had not been told that it was the great Dr Gill who preached, I should have said I had heard an Arminian."

Dr Gill's pulpit

The reader may perhaps like to look at Gill's pulpit. It has for years been used by the young men of the Pastors' College when preaching before their fellow-students. Ought they not to be *sound?*

5
John Rippon

THE mighty commentator having been followed to his grave by his attached church and a great company of ministers and Christian people, among whom he had been regarded as a great man and a prince in Israel, his church began to look around for a successor. This time as in the case of Dr Gill there was trouble in store, for there was division of opinion. Some, no doubt, as true Gillites, looked only for a solid divine, sound in doctrine, who would supply the older saints with spiritual food, while another party had an eye to the growth of the church, and to the securing to the flock the younger members of their families. They were agreed that they would write to Bristol for a probationer, and Mr John Rippon was sent to them. He was a youth of some twenty summers, of a vivacious temperament, quick and bold. The older members judged him to be too young, and too flighty; they even accused him of having gone up the pulpit stairs two steps at a time on some occasion when he was hurried – a grave offence for which the condemnation could hardly be too severe. He was only a young man, and came from an academy, and this alone was enough to make the sounder and older members afraid of him. He preached for a lengthened time on probation, and finally some forty persons withdrew because they could not agree with the enthusiastic vote by which the majority of the people elected him.

John Rippon modestly expressed his wonder that even more had not been dissatisfied, and his surprise that so large a number were agreed to call him to the pastorate. In the spirit of forbearance and brotherly love he proposed that, as these friends were seceding for conscience sake, and intended to form themselves into another church, they should be lovingly

John Rippon in his youth

dismissed with prayer and God-speed, and that, as a token of fraternal love, they should be assisted to build a meeting-house for their own convenience, and the sum of £300 should be voted to them when their church was formed and their meeting-house erected. The promise was redeemed, and Mr Rippon took part in the ordination service of the first minister. This was well done. Such a course was sure to secure the blessing of God. The church in Dean Street thus became another off-shoot from the parent stem, and with varying conditions it remains to this day (1876) as the church in Trinity Street, Borough. It is somewhat remarkable as illustrating the perversity of human judgment that the seceding friends who objected to Rippon's youth elected for their pastor Mr William Button who was younger still, being only nineteen years of age. His father, however, was a deacon under Dr Gill, and therefore no doubt the worthy youth was regarded with all the more tenderness; nor did he disappoint the hopes of his friends, for he laboured on for more than forty years with the utmost acceptance. The friends who remained with young John Rippon had no reason to regret their choice: the tide of prosperity set in and continued for half a century, and the church again came to the front in denominational affairs. The chapel in Carter Lane was enlarged, and various agencies and societies set in motion; there was, in fact, a real revival of religion in the church, though it was of that quiet style which became a Baptist church of the straiter sort. Rippon was rather clever than profound; his talents were far inferior to those of Gill, but he had more tact, and so turned his gifts to the greatest possible account. He said many smart and witty things, and his preaching was always lively, affectionate, and impressive. He was popular in the best sense of the term – beloved at home, respected abroad, and useful everywhere. Many souls were won to Jesus by his teaching, and out of these a remarkable number became themselves ministers of the gospel. The Church book abounds with records of brethren preaching before the church, as the custom was in those days.

In order to provide the denomination with information as to its own affairs, he projected the *"Baptist Register,"* and edited it for several years. Its general tone and spirit have been well brought out in a sketch by Mr Goadby in his *"Bye-paths of Baptist History."* At first sight the contents of the *Register* do not promise modern readers very dainty fare; but on a further and more careful examination, especially in the long footnotes given in some of the volumes, one discovers many tasty morsels. A few of these we now give. It will be seen, that while Dr Rippon and his friends were animated by the very laudable desire of presenting an accurate account of the Baptist denomination during the latter half of the last century, they often indulged in the freest and quaintest criticisms on ministers who were then living.

"Of *Willingham*, Cambs, we are told, 'The good man (John Rootham, the minister) has been much tried with an asthmatical complaint and other disorders, so that he seldom enjoys a day's health. But he has a considerable congregation, and about forty members.' Nicholas Gillard, the pastor of *Cullompton*, Devon, 'is eighty. His people say that his path is like that of the just, shining more and more unto the perfect day.' Daniel Sprague, the minister of *Tiverton*, enjoys a singularly robust constitution. '*He says that preaching fourteen or fifteen sermons a week strengthens his body, and invigorates his soul.*' It is reported of John Rippon, Snr, of *Upoltery*, 'that he is a man of the sweetest temper; and that good judges say he preaches better and better.' The minister of *Coventry*, John Butterworth, we learn, 'went to London to collect money in payment of the debt on the meeting-house, and bore the fatigue as well as could be expected.'

"There are two or three curious morsels from Yorkshire. The first relates to the minister at *Bradford*. 'The aged father *Crabtree* is now getting feeble, and sometimes sits down once or twice in the course of his sermon; but great savour attends his prayers and all his discourses, and he preaches with as much zeal and animation as ever.' The second refers to Mr James Shuttleworth, of *Coerling Hill*. We are told, with the most charming frankness, that this minister 'is a man of weak constitution, with a little wife and ten children, *many of them very small!*' A friend also writes of Mr William Hague, the minister of *Scarborough*: 'Our beloved pastor is advancing in years, and almost blind. He is a zealous, faithful labourer in this corner of Christ's vineyard. He has a wife and three children at home. His last year's salary amounted to £30, which is the most we ever raised him.'

"Of the other ministers who are singled out for special remark, two instances must suffice. The Rev W Clarke, of *Exeter*, is spoken of as a man remarkable for prudence and sweetness of temper. Surely Mr Clarke's modesty must have suffered some shock when his virtues were thus paraded before the whole denomination. But the most singular comment is on the Rev Thomas Mabbott, of *Biggleswade*, Beds. 'As a preacher he was much too loud and too long, a habit rarely attended with such desirable effects as ministers are ready to expect; but it is ruinous to themselves, and often creates a disgust in the minds of even a serious audience, and mars the whole service.' Poor Mr Mabbott! He had gone to his rest before this public lecturing on his defects could produce either pain or profit.

"There are two items about *deacons* that are sufficiently quaint to merit quoting. One refers to Mr John Hall, a deacon of the church at *Hamsterly*, Devon. 'He was a man never taken by surprise. However adverse any dispensation, he never said more than, "*It might have been worse.*" It was long remembered of him that when he had a crop of wheat so shaken by the wind that there was scarcely a grain of it left in the ear, upon taking hold of some, he said to the reapers, "Well, it might have been worse. *Here is good straw left for which we ought to be thankful!*"' Verily, Mr Hall was an exceptional farmer, to say the very least. The other is recorded of Mr Davey, a deacon of *Chard*. 'He had,' so we are told, with imperturbable gravity, 'nine children; and at, or near the birth of each child he was favoured with an additional cow to his worldly substance; so that he had as many cows as children, and no more!'

"The man who could pen these quaint and curious details was not destitute of humour; and one cannot but regret that only four volumes of the Register appeared. We have thereby lost many side glimpses, and some sad ones also, of the Baptist ministers and people of the close of the Eighteenth Century."

Dr Rippon also occupied himself with preparing a history of the worthies who lie buried in Bunhill Fields, and a number of subscribers' names were received, but the work never reached the press. Rippon was a busy man, and though neither a scholar nor an original thinker, his pen was seldom idle and himself never.

He will be best known as having prepared the first really good *selection of hymns* for dissenting congregations. Although a Baptist collection it was extensively used with Dr Watts' among both classes of Congregationalists. This work was an estate to its author, and he is said to have been more than sufficiently eager to push its sale. One thing we know, his presents of nicely bound copies must have been pretty frequent, for we have seen several greatly prized by their aged owners, who have showed them to us, with the remark, "The dear old doctor gave me that himself."

The happy eccentricity of the doctor's character may be illustrated by a little incident in connection with royalty. He was deputed to read an address from the dissenters to George III, congratulating him upon recovery from sickness. The doctor read on with his usual clear utterance, until coming to a passage in which there was special reference to the goodness of God, he paused and said, "Please, your majesty, we will read that again," and then proceeded with his usual cool dignity to repeat the sentence with emphasis. No other man in the deputation would have thought of doing such a thing, but from Rippon it came so naturally that no one censured him, or if they did it would have had no effect upon *him*. He was asked why he did not attend more denominational meetings and take the lead, "Why," said he, "I see the Dover coach go by my house every morning, and I notice that the leaders get most lashed." A somewhat inglorious argument for keeping in the rear.

In his later days Rippon was evidently in very comfortable circumstances, for we have often heard mention of his carriage and pair, or rather "glass coach and two horses." His congregation was one of the wealthiest within the pale of nonconformity, and always ready to aid the various societies which sprang up, especially the Baptist Foreign Mission, and a certain Baptist Itinerant Society, which we suppose to have represented the Baptist Home Mission. The Pastor occupied no mean position in the church, but ruled with dignity and discretion – perhaps ruled a little too much. "How is it, Doctor, that your church is always so peaceful?" said at much-tried brother minister. "Well, friend," said Rippon, "you see, we don't call a church meeting to consult about buying a new broom every time we want one, and we don't entreat every noisy member to make a speech about the price of the soap the floors are scrubbed with." In many of our smaller churches a want of common sense is very manifest in the management, and trouble is invited by the foolish methods of procedure.

Dr Rippon once said he had some of the best people in His Majesty's dominions in his church, and he used to add with a nod – "*and some of the worst!*" Some of the latter class seem to have got into office at one time, for they were evidently a hindrance rather than a help to the good man, though from his independent mode of doing things the hindrance did not much affect him. As well as we can remember the story of his founding the almshouses and schools in 1803, it runs as follows: The Doctor urges upon the deacons the necessity of such institutions; they do not see the urgency thereof; he pleads again, but like the deaf adder they are not to be charmed, charm he never so wisely. "The expense will be enormous, and the money cannot be raised;" this was the unceasing croak of the prudent officers. At length the Pastor says, "The money can be raised, and shall be. Why, if I don't go out next Monday and collect £500 before the evening meeting, I'll drop the proposal; but while I am sure the people will take up the matter heartily I will not be held back by you." Disputes in this case were urged in very plain language, but with no degree of bitterness, for the parties knew each other, and had too much mutual respect to make their relationships in the church depend upon a point of difference. All were agreed to put the Doctor to the test, and challenged him to produce the £500 next Monday, or cease to importune about almshouses. The worthy slow-coaches were up to time on the appointed evening, and the Doctor soon arrived. "Well, brethren," said he, "I have succeeded in collecting £300 – that is most encouraging, is it not?" "But," said two or three of them at once in a hurry, "you said you would get £500 or drop the matter, and we mean to keep you to your word." "By all means," said he, "and I mean to keep my word too, for there is £800 which the friends gave me almost without asking, and the rest is nearly all promised." The prudent officials were taken aback, but recovering themselves, they expressed their great pleasure, and would be ready to meet the pastor at any time and arrange for the expending of the funds. "No, no, my brethren," said the Doctor, "I shall not need your services. You have opposed me all along, and now I have done the work without you, you want to have your say in it to hinder me still; but neither you nor any other deacons shall plague a minister about this business. So, brethren, you can attend to something else." Accordingly, the old trust deed of the almshouses had a clause to the effect, that the pastor shall elect the pensioners, "*no deacon interfering."* The present minister had great pleasure in inducing the Charity Commissioners to expunge this clause, and give the pastor and deacons unitedly the power to select the objects of the charity.

Dr Rippon continued in the pastorate from 1773 to 1836, a period of 63 years. He outlived his usefulness, and it was a wonderful instance of divine care over the church that the old gentleman did not do it serious injury. He retained the will to govern after the capacity was gone, and he held his power over the pulpit though unable to occupy it to profit. Supplies who came to preach for him were not always allowed to officiate, and when they did, the old minister's remarks from his pew were frequently more quaint than agreeable. It is not an unqualified blessing to live to be 85. During the last few months Mr CHARLES ROOM, with the Doctor's full approbation, acted as his assistant, but he resigned upon the decease of Dr Rippon. He left with the esteem and good wishes of the church, and afterwards exercised a useful ministry at Portsea.

In 1830, six years before Dr Rippon's death, the old sanctuary in Carter Lane was closed to be pulled down for making the approaches to the present London Bridge. Due compensation was given, but a chapel could not be built in a day, and therefore, for three years the church was without a home and had to be indebted to the hospitality of other congregations. After so long a time for choice, the good deacons ought to have pitched upon a better site for the new edifice; but it is not hardly judging them when we say that they could not have discovered a worse position. If they had taken thirty years to look about them with the design of burying the church alive they could not have succeeded better. New Park Street is a low-lying sort of lane close to the bank of the River Thames, near the enormous breweries of Messrs. Barclay and Perkins, the vinegar factories of Mr Potts, and several large boiler works. The nearest way to it from the City was over Southwark bridge, *with a toll to pay.* No cabs could be had within about half-a-mile of the place, and the region was dim, dirty, and destitute, and frequently flooded by the river at high tides. Here, however, the new chapel must be built because the ground was a cheap freehold, and the authorities were destitute of enterprise, and would not spend a penny more than the amount in hand. That God in infinite mercy forbade the extinction of the church is no mitigation of the short-sightedness which thrust a respectable community of Christians into an out-of-the-way position, far more suitable for a tallow-melter's than a meeting-house. The chapel, however, was a neat, handsome, commodious, well-built edifice, and was regarded as one of the best Baptist chapels in London.

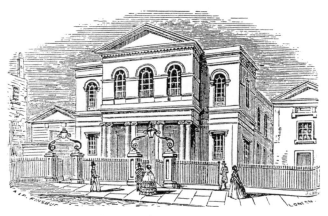

New Park Street Chapel

Dr Rippon was present at the opening of the new house in 1833, but it was very evident that, having now found a place to meet in, the next step must be to find a minister to preside over the congregation. This was no easy task, for the old gentleman, though still revered and loved, was difficult to manage in such matters. Happily, however, the deacons were supremely judicious, and having kept the interest out of all rash expenditure they also preserved it from all hasty action, and tided over affairs till the worn-out pastor passed away to his rest, and with due funereal honours was laid in that revered burying-place of Nonconformists – the cemetery of Bunhill Fields, of which it had been his ambition to become the historian and chronicler.

There are still some in the church who cherish his memory with affectionate and well-deserved reverence, and there are thousands in heaven who were led first to love the Saviour by his earnest exhortations. He quarried fresh stones, and built up the church. He moulded its thought and directed its energies. Without being great he was exceedingly useful, and the period in which he was one of the judges of our Israel was one of great prosperity in spiritual things. It was a good sixty-three years, and with the previous pastorate of Dr Gill, enabled the church to say that during one hundred and seventeen years they had been presided over by two ministers only. Those who are given to change were not numerous in the community. Short pastorates are good when ministers are feeble, but it is a great blessing when the saints are so edified that all are content, and the ministry is so owned of God that vacancies are filled up even before they are felt: in such a case change would wantonly imperil the hope of continued prosperity, and would therefore be criminal.

6
Deacon William Lepard

AS our church recognises no distinction of clergy and laity, it is not right that its history should consist entirely of the lives and labours of its pastors. It owes, under God, very much to those faithful men who have discharged the office of deacon in its midst. Most of these accomplish the labours of their sacred office with quiet unobtrusiveness, and pass away without any record of their lives being given to the world, nor are they, on this account, any the less honoured and accepted of the great Head of the Church. Occasionally, however, from remarkable circumstances or singular gifts, a deacon becomes almost as prominent as the pastor, and his life is quite a landmark in the history of the church. Such was the case with WILLIAM LEPARD, who was a member of the church for 84 years, and died in our fellowship at the age of 99. His membership ran through the pastorates of Stinton and Gill, and into the first 27 years of that of Mr Rippon. As the descendants of this eminent old disciple are still honourably connected with the Baptist body, and as the memoir written by Dr Rippon will aid our readers in forming some idea of the doctor himself, and of the manners of the church in those times, we print it almost entire, only intimating that the memoir is the closing portion of a funeral sermon preached before the Carter Lane congregation from *2 Corinthians 12:9*, and that this fact accounts for some allusions which are not of general interest, but which it would have been difficult to omit. We are glad to give a likeness of the reverend old man from a finely executed engraving in our possession: our copy falls short of the original, but hits off the likeness well.

Sketch of the Life of Mr William Lepard
By Dr Rippon

Mr William Lepard was descended of ancestors whose history had neither been emblazoned by arms, nor crested with coronets; but, though unknown to heraldry and in the courts of princes, individuals of his family were well known in the courts of the Lord's house – in thy courts, O Jerusalem! – from which a voice is heard this day, saying to all his honoured descendants, "Praise ye the Lord!"

His mother had the honour of being a member of the church when it was under the pastorate of Mr Benjamin Keach. Dr Gill has been heard to say, that she was an eminently pious woman.

Mr Lepard's grandmother also was a member of the same church: and as at her dissolution she had to review a life of ninety years, it is conceivable that she might have been one of the first members of this church, when it was formed in 1652.

Our deceased friend was born September 18, 1700, and perfectly remembered the *great storm*, in November, 1703, which was so proverbially desolating. And he had reason to do so. His father, who was in the building line, could not but know that the decayed house in which he lived must be in danger by that tremendous wind; and in the evening he said to his wife, "Let us take the child out of bed, and carry him over to Ezekiel Seward's (a Quaker who lived almost opposite),

William Lepard

for the house will be down before the morning." And according to his apprehensions, so it was. In the night the chimney fell, and bore down part of the roof which brought away the flooring, and so threw out the front; and the first sight they had, when daylight came, was the inside of their house, and the bricks and mortar lying in the street. This distinguishing providence he used to mention very circumstantially, and when he was not long since repeating it, he added, with much significance, in the words of Job's messengers, "And I only am escaped to tell thee."

Before he could well read, he was taught a number of hymns and psalms suited to the capacities of children. These were interesting to him all his days, even in later life. For them he was indebted, not to his mother only, but to his grandmother, who was no doubt of the same opinion as her pastor, Mr Keach, who, in the preface to his book of sacred hymns, says, "Since singing psalms, hymns, and spiritual songs is God's ordinance, 'tis [evidently] the duty of parents and heads of families to instruct their children therein, as well as to teach them to read; for, by learning sacred hymns, they may be taken up before their parents are aware with the matter therein contained."

Besides the advantages he received at home, his mother availed herself of other opportunities for his knowing the ways of the Lord more perfectly. She sent him to be instructed with other children at the old meeting-house, on the spot where the Rev John Townsend's, at Rotherhithe, now stands. So great was the number of young persons who attended there every Saturday afternoon, that two ministers at the same time met them, and taught them the Assembly's Catechism.

At about fourteen years of age, one day coming from school, he went to play with the other lads under the scaffold on which his father was at work. He had but just come from under it when it fell, and his father with it, who was killed on the spot, or at least did not speak afterwards. His mother, now left a widow, felt her loss. He has informed us with pleasure that she was "a widow indeed." She kept a shop, and so did Mrs Stinton, the pastor's wife; but, notwithstanding she was a widow, she had a widow's mite for the poor, especially for poor Christians. This circumstance our deceased friend has sometimes mentioned with a grateful exultation.

But though the father was removed, the son was left, and much was he the solace of his mother. Three or four days after his father's death a respectable bricklayer applied to the bereaved woman, and offered to teach her son his trade if she thought he would like it, and make him free of the city. The offer was accepted. "But," said the mother, who was not indifferent where her son went to hear the Word, nor whether he was a churchman or dissenter, "*you must, sir, let my son go to meeting with me.*" He agreed to it, and was as good as his word.

She experimentally knew the value of the means of grace, and longed that they might be gracious and saving means to her son. Though he had felt some serious concern at about ten years of age, religion had yet made no lasting impression on his mind. But when somewhat more than two years of his apprenticeship had expired, as he was grinding a broad chisel, which they call a brick-axe, with his back against a wall, and his feet on the frame in which the stone turned, the stone caught his apron, entangled the axe, drew him after it and cut his clothes and the flesh of his thigh in an awful manner, to the very bone, so that his life was in great danger. In this condition he was taken home to his mother's, and confined to his bed, which he and others feared would be his death-bed. While his body was in this imminent danger, it pleased the God of all grace to lead him into a serious consideration of the dangerous condition of his soul. His mother and the pious women who came to comfort her embraced this opportunity to converse faithfully and affectionately with him, respecting his malady as a sinner, and the remedy so gloriously exhibited in the gospel. His concern was increased, and he felt more on account of his soul than of his body. And after many tears had been shed over him and many prayers offered for him, he was helped to begin fervently to pray for himself. He wrestled with God "for the life of his soul," and praying breath was not spent in vain. The Lord sent him relief from a passage of Scripture exactly suited to his case, which I have read to you as our text – "My grace is sufficient for thee: for my strength is made perfect in weakness." He did not now more consciously feel the weakness of his body than he did the depravity of his soul, but he cherished a hope that the Lord would save the one from death, and the other from sin and everlasting misery. As this text "dwelt on his mind" and "sometimes filled him with joy," he mentioned it to his mother and to several of the godly people who came to see him, and he "felt increasing satisfaction," I use his own words, "in thinking of the work of Christ, the influence of the Holy Spirit, and salvation from sin and punishment."

Some time after his recovery, his mother said to him, "Son, I would have you go to our minister, and talk with him." He complied, it seems, in the simplicity of his heart, not intending what followed. When he had told his case, Mr Stinton encouraged him to go before the church, and relate the same to them. This he did – was soon after baptised with three other persons, and then received into full communion by laying on of the hands of the pastor, according to the practice of the church at that time. He joined this church in the year 1717, perhaps in the spring of that year. Mr Stinton died February 11, 1718, having first been a teacher in the church, and then pastor for thirteen or fourteen years.

After Mr Lepard's apprenticeship had expired, and he was arriving at an age when one should wish young persons to make their arrangements for life, his master, who had formed a great respect for him, contemplating a retirement from business, came and asked him if he knew of any person that would stand in his place. But when he found that the benevolent man intended the situation for himself, tears of joy and thankfulness (for he was always affectionate and grateful) rolled down his cheeks; and in mentioning this circumstance to me, he said, "Well they might, for it was a trade, as business then was, worth hundreds a year." This auspicious providence became the happy means of bringing up his family in comfort and credit.

Mr William Anderson, one of our deacons, having been sent into the work of the ministry by this church, Mr Lepard was appointed in his room. Our church minutes of May 2, 1743, say that he was unanimously chosen at that meeting. Twenty-four days after the choice, namely "Thursday, May 26," Dr Gill writes, "was appointed for the ordination of him; on which day the church met, and he was ordained into his office." Of that choice which was made by the church, and of this ordination which was the act of the pastor, I have never heard that they repented. For though in earlier days, the cares of a family and the multiplicity of business "in city, town, or country," as he sometimes expressed it, precluded him from serving the church according to the affectionate desires of his heart – he entered on his office by instituting, in a respectful manner, an inquiry into the circumstances of his pastor and of the church, which terminated in the advantage of the whole, and he was assisted afterwards, under his involuntary omissions, by the wise efforts of his wife, a member of the church, and one of the best of women. It was his honour and the happiness of the whole church, that Mrs Lepard had talent, and made time to assist her husband in his office. Not by name, but in her conduct, she was, until her death, a deaconess, as Phoebe is called.

Not many years after the death of Mrs Lepard, the sight of the widowed husband began to fail, and he relinquished business in favour of his second son, in whose family he lived many years at Rotherhithe, a little below Globe Stairs. This was his residence when I came to town in 1772. And here it was that I freely conversed with him respecting the affairs of this church, and received his counsels. He had now passed the first stage of Christianity, which they call comfort; and the second, which has been denominated conflict; and was at this time arrived at the third, the stage of contemplation. In this situation of leisure, as he could not see to read, when the weather would permit, he spent seven or eight hours a day in his garden, about a quarter of a mile from his dwelling: he was there sometimes at five o'clock in the morning, and frequently enjoyed on this spot days of unspeakable bliss. In this peaceful retreat also, I have met and happily conversed with him.

His vacant hours at home were well employed in the duties of seriousness and cheerfulness. Religion always appeared in a pleasing garb as dressed by him. Here the daughter-in-law found the care of bringing up a family alleviated by his counsels, by his countenance, and his conduct. When children were childish, he used to say to his daughter, "Let us remember we were children once – they will make brave men and women by-and-bye." His grandchildren surrounding his feet would listen and learn from him the hymns and little poems which he had been taught when a child.

But while he was thus pleasingly communicative and naturally disposed to make all around him happy, he did not think himself too old to learn, and therefore engaged his daughter-in-law and her children to read to him the Word of God, and the writings of the late Dr Gill, to whose works he was partial in a very high degree. The younger branches of the family recollect how fond he was of the *Epistles of John*, which they read over to him "many and many a time." With a heart so much assimilated to that of the aged and holy apostle, it is no wonder that these epistles were dear to him. He breathed love and gratitude.

It is worthy, I think, of peculiar observation, that neither the distance of his habitation, nor the dimness of his sight, hindered him from being with us in the house of God. With his staff in one hand, and the other behind his back, he walked from below Rotherhithe church to London Bridge every Lord's Day, erect as in his youth, with a countenance always in his favour; multitudes saying as he passed, "What a fine old man!" This practice he continued until he was in the ninetieth year of his age, when it will not seem strange that he felt increasing weakness, and perceived that the walk to meeting was rather more than he could take with pleasure. This opened the way to a change of residence, nearer this place of worship, by the tender care of his eldest son, who placed him under the wing of a respectable aged matron in Blackman Street, in the Borough.

It was about this time, I think, that his children and grandchildren, in looking at the term of ninety years, naturally concluded that the time drew near, when the aged saint must die; and believing that the first class of duties we owe belongs to God, and the second to our parents, they determined to have a family meeting for the purpose of expressing their most dutiful affection to him before his death. The day was fixed, and the Grove-house at Camberwell was the place appointed for the meeting. The day arrived. His children and descendants were all in health, and they were all present, those who used the distant seas not excepted – they were thirty-nine in number. I was the only person present, not a relative, and made the fortieth. The sight I shall never forget. What an assemblage! I saw the great-grandchildren, beauteous vernal buds. The grandchildren were full blown roses. The children had passed into summer, not having entirely lost the beauties of spring; but the countenance and conduct, the cheerfulness and piety of their aged father, on that day, exhibited a man – a holy man –

"Crowned with perpetual harvest."

Sitting by his side, when the table was covered, I said to him, Sir, it falls on you to ask a blessing. He rose like a patriarch, at the head of his family, and in these words, taken as they flowed from his lips, he addressed the Supreme Majesty:

"Ever-living and ever-loving God! Thou hast been pleased to bless thine unworthy dust with this family: – O Lord, bless them! He would give them all into thine hands. Bless them in their bodies, and bless them in their souls; and may great grace be upon them all! We now beg thy blessing upon what is before us, that it may be refreshing to us, and that we may glorify thee, the Father of all our mercies, for Jesus' sake." Every voice said, Amen.

Dinner and the services of the table being over, one present waved his hand, at which the whole company were on their feet, and humbly representing the rest, he said, "We look at our venerable father and thank him for his care of us in youth, his advice to us in riper years, and his affectionate concern for us to this hour. May his last days be his best days!"

Many years antecedent to this, there is sufficient reason to believe that this honoured man had been advancing in purity and in bliss, nor was his career less holy and happy afterwards. He was not among the chilling and disheartening circle of aged professors, compared by Mr Toplady to decayed mile stones, which have lost their inscription, and answer no end in the world but that of mortifying the traveller, who looks to read how far he has to go to reach his journey's end, but looks in vain. No man more cheerfully said than Mr Lepard, from time to time, "By the grace of God, I am what I am." But we ourselves subjoin, that the grace of God which was bestowed upon him was not in vain. A decayed mile stone? No; though almost ninety years of age when he came to reside in this neighbourhood, he appeared in general as lively in his soul as any young Christian in the church. Our Lord's Day morning prayer meetings, at half-past nine, will witness this. How constant was his attendance! He was often present one of the first. At these beneficial services, his very countenance did good to younger Christians, and to persons more advanced. At one time, as he entered, I heard him say, "Peace be to you, my brethren, in the name of the Lord." At another time he breathed this language, "My feet shall stand within thy gates, O Jerusalem!" He mostly came among us with cheerfulness, and always with solemnity. How animating has it been to the church and the congregation, to see the son lead the father, whose eyes were dim by reason of age, through the aisle to the pew, and to see the venerable man take his seat! How have our hearts moved and melted while witnessing his devotion in the house of the Lord, and especially at the Lord's Table!

But his piety, conspicuous abroad, was also eminent at home. There he uttered not the language of murmuring and suspicion. The voice of fretfulness, peevishness, and the other attendant frailties and crimes of old age, were far from his tents. He was condescending to the young, affectionate to his children, attentive to his friends, courteous to all, and a most rigid observer of the truth in all his intercourse with the world and the church. Though, I think, he was somewhat too backward in the performance of public prayer, he was a pattern in private prayer. Morning, noon, and night, he constantly attempted to draw near to God, and when, through age, he could not retire for the performance of this holy duty, those who were around him withdrew and left him alone. Of late years, it was pretty much his custom to use his voice distinctly in this service; and it is well known that he was mighty in prayer through the power of the Holy Ghost. He finished his day with prayer, and entered on the next with praise. To all this I must yet add, that during the last eight or nine years of his life, from ninety years of age and upwards, his days were happier than they were long, being eminently unclouded and blissful. The intervals of prayer he continually filled up with praise. Two, three, or four hymns a day, unless he was ill, which was seldom the case, were cheerfully sung by him; and sometimes he was singing almost all the day. Three of his favourite hymns and psalms, which he sung much more often than the rest, were these: – the twenty-third psalm by Dr Watts, beginning with,

> "The Lord my shepherd is,
> I shall be well supplied."

And that hymn in which is this remarkable verse –

> "Hail, great Immanuel, all divine:
> In thee thy Father's glories shine!
> Thou brightest, sweetest, fairest one,
> That eyes have seen, or angels known!"

And this also –

> "Come, Holy Spirit, heavenly dove,
> With all thy quickening powers;" etc.

What has been hitherto related concerning our deceased friend is pretty generally known in most of our little circles, and has been sometimes repeated in our parlours; it cannot therefore possibly be considered in the light of posthumous commendation, lavished with a prodigal hand over the ashes of the dead, to which the public voice would have denied its sanction while he was living; but all my friends, and every member of the church, will estimate this report, made in honour of the grace of God, as a testimony of sober praise to which our deceased friend and father had a legitimate claim; for his life had indeed been a living testimony. He has also left a dying testimony, which I shall now state if you will indulge me with your patience.

You will be glad to hear that his powers of memory were good until the last day but one of his life. About a fortnight before he died, I called, and saw him happy. He had just finished singing one of his hymns as I came to the door. A few days after, as I am informed, he felt a pain in his back for about five minutes, which it seems was all the pain he endured. Debility came on; his case was perfectly understood; medical assistance was administered with equal kindness and skill by a respectable member of his family, who prudently gave an intimation to the other affectionate relatives that nine or ten days would terminate the complaint, which was a dissolution of the blood. The eighth day of the ten arrived; and then Saturday, the ninth of the ten. In the morning of it, his eldest son and daughter, attending his bedside, witnessed the happiness of the good man, whose language, now often repeated, was, "Bless the Lord, O my soul, and forget not all his benefits." "Thou hast dealt bountifully with me." He then distinctly and at length recounted the Lord's dealings with him in providence, and his kindness as the God of grace. He afterwards spake with much energy of the love of God, who passed by fallen angels, and before all worlds elected a certain number of men to salvation out of every nation, and kindred, and tongue, and people; "Yea," said he, "and chose them *to* himself, and *for* himself, gave them to his Son to redeem, and by his Holy Spirit makes them meet for the inheritance of the saints in light," adding, "I hope you are no strangers to these things, on which your dear minister is so often speaking to you." He expatiated on the love of Christ, as enduring the cross and despising the shame, before he sat down at his Father's right hand. After remaining a few minutes composed and still, he broke out in one of the most sublime and beautiful prayers. He prayed for himself, that the enemy might be as still as a stone, while he passed over Jordan; he prayed for his sons; for his daughter, then by his bedside; for each of his grandchildren, and their children, that they might be a generation to serve the Lord. In the afternoon he spoke in adoring strains of the covenant of grace, and expressed his joy in prospect of the latter-day glory, and of Christ as presenting the church to his Father without spot, or wrinkle, or any such thing. At intervals he sung Hallelujah; and indeed his room seemed to be the antechamber of glory.

This Saturday evening I had the pleasure to visit him again. I found him somewhat exhausted by much exertion in conversing with his children one after another, in the different parts of the day; but his recollection was perfect, and with detail he continued to relate, for about half-an-hour, some of the kind providences of God towards him in early life, which he had several times mentioned to me when he was in full health, and now, as circumstantially as ever. "I have been talking to my son William," said he, "who has known my life from the fifteenth year of his age till now." But I dismiss the whole of his conversation, except one thing.

Who could have borne to hear the love and gratitude of this ancient and apostolic man, when with his dying lips he thanked his son for all his kindness to him, saying, "Son, you have been a Joseph to me."

I turn from the subject a moment, and request that I may become an angel of entreaty to all the young people in this assembly, especially to those who have praying and godly parents. I beseech you, in the name of our Lord Jesus Christ, that as opportunity may offer, you will each of you, with duty, affection, and gratitude, aspire to be a Joseph to your aged parents.

It was about seven o'clock in the evening, when I proposed the following questions to him: his answers were pencilled by a person at his bedside, as they came from his lips:

Q. Are you in pain, sir?

A. I am not, sir, blessed be God. This is a comfort, sir, a very great one.

Q. Do you know, sir, what day it will be tomorrow?

A. Yes, Lord's Day; the Lord crown the day with his blessing! – What, sir, are there any people then to join you tomorrow, to join the church?

Q. No, sir, not tomorrow; but you joined it once, sir?

A. Yes, and a charming day it was, blessed be God. He has given me a name and a place in his house, better than that of sons and daughters: and that was a charming day, sir, when he said to me, "My grace is sufficient for thee, for my strength is made perfect in weakness." And it was so. It was so.

Q. Do any of the truths and promises which comforted you formerly, support you now, sir?

A. Yes, the first words are good now; he does strengthen me, he does support me. I cannot wait upon him now as I could then: I cannot do as I would. I wish for more light, and more life, and more love: though I have lost my sight, I can look back and see the way by which he has brought me, and I can look forward too, sir. Oh, that's comfortable!

Q. I am afraid, sir, I tire you?

A. Oh no, sir, I am not tired, if you are not; I am willing to speak, if you are willing to hear.

Q. If you should, within a few hours, sir, meet Dr Gill in glory?

A. Aye, and my mother, and grandmother, and multitudes of precious souls besides, and the precious Jesus.

After giving him a little time I proposed one question more.

Q. Have you, sir, any fear of death?

A. No fear of death; I am not afraid at all; I know the Lord to be my strength, my portion, and my God. "The Lord is my portion, saith my soul; therefore will I hope in him."

This text he repeated, and then said, "He will not forsake me now, he has given me his word he will not; I have his gospel for it."

So far was he from being exercised with the fear of death, that in the forenoon of this very day, the last day of his reason, and the last but one of his life, he had been most pleasantly singing several verses, of which these are some of the lines –

"The grave is a refining pot," etc.

And when he came to this part of them,

"The flesh shall lose its dross,
And like the sun shall rise,"

he lifted up his hands with every expression of joy; and finding that he could not sing all the verses through as distinctly as he had done before, speaking of the aged servant in the house, he said, "she can help me out." Here was vigour at *ninety-nine* years of age! Here was bliss on the very shores of death. How gracious was God to this his servant! Was not this departing in peace, having seen God's salvation? My heart and voice said, "Let me die the death of the righteous, and let my last end be like his." With this desire, assured that God would safely convey him over the river, I pressed his dying hand to my lips, and he as affectionately kissed mine in return. "The Lord be with you," said he; I replied, "and with your spirit!"

and so we parted on Saturday evening about nine o'clock. And this I believe was the last regular conversation that he held with any person, and a wish being expressed that he might be kept still all the night, nothing particular transpired after that time.

I called to see him between the morning and afternoon services of the Lord's Day, and perceived that he was fast going the way of all the earth. His eldest son, a deacon of this church, spent the afternoon of the day with him waiting to see his last; and he frequently heard him say – Hallelujah, Hallelujah, Hallelujah; and as far as he could interpret, he thought his dying father was saying or singing in death,

> "Glory, honour, praise, and power,
> Be unto the Lamb for ever,
> Jesus Christ is our Redeemer!
> Hallelujah!"

Which was the last word he attempted to articulate; and thus he sweetly fell asleep in Jesus, just as we were going out of meeting in the afternoon, Lord's Day, January 20, 1799, in the 99th year of his age, having been a member of this church about eighty-two years.

7
Three Short Pastorates

THE next pastor of our Church was Mr (now Dr) JOSEPH ANGUS, a gentleman whose career since he left us to become secretary of the Baptist Missionary Society, and afterwards the tutor of Stepney Academy, now Regent's Park College, has rendered his name most honourable among living Baptists. He is one of the foremost classical scholars, and is a member of the committee for producing a revised version of the Holy Scriptures. He is the author of those standard books, "*The Bible Handbook,*" "*The Handbook of the English Tongue,*" and "*Handbook of English Literature.*" We cannot better describe his coming to New Park Street than by quoting a part of the paper in the Church book, which was read by Mr Gale, one of the deacons, at the ordination service, held December 27th, 1837.

"With so aged a minister as Dr Rippon, declining in mental energy and bodily strength, it was not to be wondered at that, during his latter years, the church should be reduced in numbers, as well of members as of general hearers – but when there is added the circumstances of our having been turned out of the place in which we had worshipped for upwards of seventy years, and that for about three years we had to seek accommodation from the kindness of other churches, assembling at different times in Unicorn Yard, in Mile's Lane, and in Dean Street – such of the friends present as are acquainted with our history, will readily believe that those who have taken a management in the affairs of the church have often felt their hearts sinking within them at the fear of its entire dissolution.

"For several years we laid various plans, but they were frustrated. We had set our minds on various ministers, but we were not allowed the opportunity of inviting them. We felt for *our* section of the church as though *that* were the most important; but by our disappointments and by the placing of those ministers over other sections of the church which required to be provided for, we were taught that the great Head of the Church watched over the whole flock, and under this consideration we were encouraged to hope that the time would come when *we also* should be cared for, and we were led to believe that his care would be manifested to us in the most suitable time.

"As the most effectual way of obtaining our wishes a *special* Prayer Meeting was appointed to be held every alternate week. 'Prayer made the darkened cloud withdraw.' The name of our dear brother, Joseph Angus, was in a short time mentioned to us as that of a zealous and studious young minister; and what was of most importance, as of a young man of ardent piety. He was at that time pursuing his studies at Edinburgh, where he was expected to continue until the end of April. He was written to with a request that he would supply for us during the month of May. His reply to this request did not arrive for several days, but when we received it we were encouraged by the words in which it commences. They were these: 'My unwillingness to make even the most trifling movement until some effort had been made to ascertain the Divine will has prevented my answering your letter earlier.'

"The church had sought by prayer – the answer was given after prayer; and the letter concluded by leading us to expect him on the second or third Sabbath in May.

"A severe illness arising from a winter session at the University of more than usual labour, and the subsequent illness and death of a dear sister, compelled him to postpone his visit, and he did not arrive amongst us until the first of October. We, however, continued our special Prayer Meetings for Divine direction, under our peculiar circumstances. Mr Angus was not known to any of us; we had, therefore, no personal predilections in his favour. We had sought a pastor from the great Shepherd of the church, and we trusted to him to supply us with one.

"On the 1st of October Mr Angus came among us as a stranger, but he was no stranger at the close of the next week. We had heard good reports of him, and we had the gratification of finding all our expectations more than realised. Having been favoured with his labours on two Sabbath-days and also at our weekly and special prayer meetings, we hesitated not to request that (after he should have been at Oxford, where he had promised to supply for a month) he would renew his visit to us for three months. His discourses to us, however, on the third and fourth Sabbaths in October, and his visits among the people so convinced us that our prayers had been heard, and that God had sent us a 'Pastor according to his own heart, who should feed us with knowledge and understanding' that we could no longer content ourselves with our previous invitation, but determined before he went to Oxford to call a special meeting of the church. It was numerously attended, and after solemn prayer and serious deliberation, it was resolved without a dissentient voice, and we believe with an entirely unanimous feeling, to invite him to become the pastor of this church."

The union thus formed was confirmed by the divine blessing, and cemented by mutual esteem. During Mr Angus' pastorate the privilege of communing at the Lord's Table was extended to members of other churches, whether baptised or not, and this was done quietly and without division, though a considerable minority did not agree with it. The church remains a community of baptised believers, and its constitution will not admit any persons into its membership but those immersed upon personal profession of faith in the Lord Jesus; but it does not attempt to judge the order and discipline of other churches, and has fellowship in the breaking of bread with all churches which form parts of the mystical body of Christ; thus it endeavours to fulfil at the same time the duties of purity and love.

In December, 1839, the Baptist Missionary Society invited Mr Angus to become its Home Secretary. The members were deeply grieved, and passed a resolution expressive of their indignation, mentioning among other reasons why they should not be robbed of their pastor that "when this meeting contemplates that within twelve months nearly fifty members have been added through their pastor's instrumentality, and that from the number of enquirers there is a prospect of still larger additions, they cannot but appeal to the Christian feelings of their brethren on the Committee of the Baptist Missionary Society, requesting them to consider whether they are not inflicting a wound on the church which no circumstances can justify." Corporations, however, have few bowels of compassion, and so after various interim arrangements the beloved minister was removed from his people. A sense of the importance of the Missionary Society, and the fact that after much deliberation the committee could not discover anyone else about whom they could be at all unanimous, were the motives which led him to leave the church, to the deep regret of all the members.

After the removal of Dr Angus the church was happily directed to hear Mr JAMES SMITH, whose useful ministry in Cheltenham was an abundant guarantee that he was likely to prove the right man to collect a congregation in New Park Street. He was pastor for about eight and a half years, from 1841 to 1850, and then returned to Cheltenham, from which many of his best friends are of the opinion that he ought never to have removed. He was a man of slender education, but of great natural ability, sound in the faith, intensely earnest, and a ready speaker. He is the author of a very large number of little books, which are published at a cheap rate by Milner and Sowerby, of Halifax, and have been the means of numberless conversions, as well as of the comfort and edification of

James Smith

believers. Few men have ever been more useful than he. Happily for us he kept a diary of his own inward experience, and we cannot better illustrate the course of his ministry than by quoting from it those passages which have a direct reference to his labours in London.

"*1841 November 9th* – Having received an invitation from the church at New Park Street, London, after much prayer and searching of heart, I have this night resigned my office as pastor of the Church in Salem. This is a painful crisis in my history. I feel it deeply, but I trust I am acting in accordance with the will of God."

"*1842 April 10th* – When I left Cheltenham and came to reside in London, I found the church in a very low state, and the congregation very small. I trust the Lord brought me here. Many more attend the Word, and the people profess to profit; some are impressed, but the place does not fill as Salem did. O for a revival! My path has been outwardly prosperous, but inwardly painful. I never was tried with a small congregation before, but I am now. Lord, how long? When I look around me I see a beautiful chapel, a dense population, but no spirit of hearing. When I look forward there appears to be a *mist* before my eyes, and I cannot see my way. The people are greatly encouraged, but I often feel perplexed, I will therefore wait upon my God."

"*1842 November 19th* – My fortieth birthday ... In the church we are at peace, and the affection of the people appears to increase. I hope that their spirituality grows also. The good work goes on, though not so rapidly as I could wish. But if God is with us, if we simply aim to please him, he will bless us, and crown us with success."

"*1843 February* – During the past year, sixty-six members were added to the church, and the congregation increased three-fold. The Lord's people say they are profited, and they appear to be much attached to my person and ministry. The prayer meeting is crowded, and some souls are converted. But I want to see greater things. I am by no means satisfied."

"*1844 November 19th* – The church now increases faster than it has done since I have been its pastor, but not so fast as I wish to see it. I try a variety of means, and feel determined to leave no stone unturned for its welfare and advantage. I am surrounded by a great many young people, very hopeful characters. This encourages me, and I continue to plead with God for many of them by name, and I preach to them monthly. O to have many of them given unto me as my joy and crown of rejoicing in the day of the Lord!"

"*1846 November 19th* – We have had many converted to God under the preaching of the Word, and the church now numbers 450. To God alone be all the praise!"

"*1847 November 19th* – The church increases, the congregation is larger than it has been since I have been in London, and my ministry is blessed to the conversion of sinners, especially my monthly sermons to the young. I bless God that I ever began this practice, and that I have persevered in it until now."

"*1848 July* – We have had many removals of late and not so many additions, so that I begin to feel sad and somewhat unsettled, for I feel as if I could not live, much less be happy, if souls are not constantly brought to God. I have spoken to the church on the subject from *Psalm 74:9: 'We see not our signs.'* After noticing God's condescension in granting signs and tokens under the former dispensation, and the design of them, I endeavoured to set forth the signs we desire to witness. Signs of life imparted to those who are dead in sin, liveliness in the saints, and a revival of religion in the church and congregation. Observing, 'we see not our signs,' for few are added to the church, few are found deciding for God, few are enquiring the way to Zion, few are found properly affected with the state of the world and the church. Our prayer meetings are not thronged. The spirit of wrestling prayer does not appear; the Lord's arm is not laid bare. The language of my soul must now be,

'I will wait for the Lord, who hideth himself from the house of Israel, and I will look for him.' O that he would soon appear, and put forth his power with the Word!"

"*1849 October* – For a considerable time I have felt an oppression on my chest, and great difficulty in breathing; last week I consulted a doctor upon it. He advised me to leave London as soon as I could, and get into the country, as my lungs require a purer air. This puts an entirely new face on my circumstances. I am seeking wisdom from God: I cannot doubt but he will guide me."

"*1850 February* – I have written my resignation of office, and laid it before the deacons. It is a serious and important step which I have taken. I trust I have taken it in a proper spirit, and from a right motive. My mind is now calm and peaceful, the agitation from which I have long been suffering is at an end, and I feel as if I could now leave the matter with the Lord."

"When my resignation was accepted, the church passed a very kind and affectionate resolution, regretting that I felt it necessary to take such a step, but as I had rested it pretty much on the state of my health, they did not feel that they could refuse to accede to my wishes. I cannot say that I have laboured in vain here, for many souls have been converted, some backsliders have been restored, and between 400 and 500 members have been added to the church during my pastorate of eight years. Many of my poor people deeply feel the step which I have felt it my duty to take, and I have received very affectionate letters from several of them. May they soon be favoured with a pastor more suitable and efficient than I have been."

Mr Smith built up in Cheltenham the strong working church now meeting in Cambray Chapel, which was erected by his exertions. When he was lying upon his dying bed the church at the Tabernacle sent him a heartily affectionate letter, and gratefully reminded him of all the blessing which the Lord had bestowed upon many souls by his means. To this we received a delightful answer assuring us that our words had greatly cheered him. He died in 1861, and an account of an interview with him is contained in No. 491 of the "*Metropolitan Tabernacle Pulpit.*" It may interest the reader if we include it in our pages. "I saw this week the former pastor of this church, Mr James Smith, of Cheltenham. About a year ago, he was struck with paralysis, and one half of his body is dead. But yet I have seldom seen a more cheerful man in the full heyday of strength. I had been told that he was the subject of very fearful conflicts at times; so after I had shaken hands with him, I said, 'Friend Smith, I hear you have many doubts and fears!' 'Who told you that?' said he, 'for I have none.' 'Never have any? why, I understood you had many conflicts.' 'Yes,' he said, 'I have many *conflicts*, but I have no *doubts;* I have many wars within, but I have no fears. Who could have told you that? I hope I have not led anyone to think that it is a hard battle, but the victory is sure.' Then he said in his own way, 'I am just like a packet that is all ready to go by train, packed, corded, labelled, paid for, and on the platform, waiting for the express to come by and take me to glory. I wish I could hear the whistle now.'"

In July, 1851, the church invited the Rev WILLIAM WALTERS, of Preston, now of Birmingham, to become the Pastor, but as he understood the deacons to intimate to him that his ministry was not acceptable, he tendered his resignation, and although requested to remain, he judged it more advisable to remove to Halifax in June 1853, thus closing a ministry of two years. These changes sadly diminished the church and marred its union. The clouds gathered heavily and no sunlight appeared.

8
C H Spurgeon

IT is not to be expected that we should write the story of our own personal ministry: this must be left to other pens, if it be thought worthwhile to write it at all. We could not turn these pages into an autobiography, nor could we very well ask anyone else to write about us, and therefore we shall simply give bare facts, and extracts from the remarks of others.

On one of the last Sabbaths of the month of December, 1853, C H Spurgeon, being then nineteen years of age, preached in New Park Street Chapel, in response to an invitation which, very much to his surprise, called him away from a loving people in Waterbeach, near Cambridge, to supply a London pulpit. The congregation was a mere handful. The chapel seemed very large to the preacher, and very gloomy, but he stayed himself on the Lord, and delivered his message from *James 1:17*. There was an improvement even on the first evening, and the place looked more cheer-ful; the text was, "They are without fault before the throne of God."

In answer to earnest requests, C H Spurgeon agreed to preach in London on the first, third, and fifth Sundays in January, 1854, but before the last of these Sabbaths he had received an invitation, dated January 25, inviting him to occupy the pulpit for six months upon probation. The reply to this invitation will be found entire in Mr Pike's "*Sketches of Nonconformity in Southwark.*"

The six months' probation was never fulfilled, for there was no need. The place was filling, the prayer meetings were full of power, and conver-sion was going on. A requisition for a special meeting, signed by fifty of the male members was sent in to the deacons on April 12, and according to the Church book it was, on April 19, resolved unanimously, "that we tender our brother, the Rev C H Spurgeon, a most cordial and affectionate invitation forthwith to become pastor of this church, and we pray that the result of his services may be owned of God with an outpouring of the Holy Spirit and a revival of religion in our midst; that it may be fruitful in the conversion of sinners and in the edification of those that believe."

To this there was but one reply, and it was therefore answered in the affirmative in a letter dated April 28, 1854, also inserted in Mr Pike's book, which can be had of our publishers.

C H Spurgeon

In a very short time the congregation so multiplied as to make the chapel in the evening, when the gas was burning, like the black-hole of Calcutta. One evening in 1854 the preacher exclaimed, "By faith the walls of Jericho fell down, and by faith this wall at the back shall come down, too." An aged and prudent deacon in somewhat domineering terms observed to him, at the close of the sermon. "Let us never hear of that again." "What do you mean?" said the preacher, "you will hear no more about it when it is done, and therefore the sooner you set about doing it, the better." A meeting was held, and a fund was commenced, and in due course the vestries and schools were laid into the chapel and a new schoolroom was erected along the side of the chapel, with windows which could be let down, to allow those who were seated in the school to hear the preacher. While this was being done, worship was carried on at Exeter Hall, from February 11, 1855, to May 27 of the same year. At this time paragraphs began to appear in the papers announcing that the Strand was blocked up by crowds who gathered to hear a young man in Exeter Hall. Remarks of no very flattering character appeared in various journals, and the multitude was thereby increased. Caricatures, such as "Brimstone and Treacle" adorned the print-sellers' windows, the most ridiculous stories were circulated, and the most cruel falsehoods invented, but all these things worked together for good. The great Lord blessed the Word more and more to the conversion of the hearers, and Exeter Hall was thronged throughout the whole time of our sojourn.

Brimstone and Treacle

To return to New Park Street, enlarged though it was, resembled the attempt to put the sea into a teapot. We were more inconvenienced than ever. To turn many hundreds away was the general if not the universal necessity, and those who gained admission were but little better off, for the packing was dense in the extreme, and the heat something terrible even to remember. Our enemies continued to make our name more and more known by penny pamphlets and letters in the papers, which all tended to swell the crowd. More caricatures appeared, and among the rest "Catch-'em-alive-O!"

In June 1856 we were again at Exeter Hall, preaching there in the evening and at the chapel in the morning; but this was felt to be inconvenient, and therefore in August a fund was commenced to provide for the erection of a larger house of prayer. Meanwhile the Exeter Hall proprietors intimated that they were unable to let their hall continuously to one congregation, and therefore

Catch-'em-alive-O!

we looked about us for another place. Most opportunely a large hall, in the Royal Surrey Gardens, was just completed for the monster concerts of M. Jullien, and, with some trembling at the magnitude of the enterprise, this hall was secured for Sabbath evenings.

We find the following entry in the Church book: "Lord's Day, October 19, 1856. On the evening of this day, in accordance with the resolution passed at the Church meeting October 6th, the church and congregation assembled to hear our pastor, in the Music Hall of the Royal Surrey Gardens. A very large number of persons (about 7000) were assembled on that occasion, and the service was commenced in the usual way, by singing, reading the Scriptures, and prayer. Just, however, after our Pastor had commenced his prayer, a disturbance was caused (as it is supposed, by some evil-disposed persons acting in concert), and the whole congregation were seized with a sudden panic. This caused a fearful rush to the doors, particularly from the galleries. Several persons, either in consequence of their heedless haste, or from the extreme pressure of the crowd behind, were thrown down on the stone steps of the north-west staircase, and were trampled on

Surrey Gardens Music Hall

by the crowd pressing upon them. The lamentable result was that seven persons lost their lives, and twenty-eight were removed to the hospitals seriously bruised and injured. Our pastor not being aware that any loss of life had occurred, continued in the pulpit, endeavouring by every means in his power to alleviate the fear of the people, and was successful to a very considerable extent. In attempting to renew the service, it was found that the people were too excited to listen to him, and the service was closed, and the people who remained dispersed quietly. This lamentable circumstance produced very serious effects on the nervous system of our pastor. He was entirely prostrated for some days, and compelled to relinquish his preaching engagements. Through the great mercy of our heavenly Father, he was, however, restored so as to be able to occupy the pulpit in our own chapel on Sunday, October 31st, and gradually recovered his wonted health and vigour. 'The Lord's name be praised!'

"The church desire to note this event in their minutes, and to record their devout thankfulness to God that in this sad calamity the lives of their beloved pastor, the deacons, and members were all preserved; and also with the hope that our heavenly Father from this seeming evil may produce the greatest amount of real lasting good."

This was the way in which this great affliction was viewed by our church; but we had, in addition to the unutterable pain of the whole catastrophe, to bear the wicked accusations of the public press. We will give only one specimen; it is taken from a popular newspaper which has long been most friendly to us, and therefore we will not mention names. In the days of its ignorance it said – "Mr Spurgeon is a preacher who hurls damnation at the heads of his sinful hearers. Some men there are who, taking their precepts from Holy Writ, would beckon erring souls to a rightful path with fair words and gentle admonition; Mr Spurgeon would take them by the nose and bully them into religion. Let us set up a barrier to the encroachments and blasphemies of men like Spurgeon, saying to them, 'Thus far shalt thou come and no further;' let us devise some powerful means which shall tell to the thousands who now stand in need of enlightenment, – This man, in his own opinion, is a righteous Christian, but in ours nothing more than a ranting charlatan. We are neither straight-laced nor Sabbatarian in our sentiments: but we would keep apart, widely apart, the theatre and the church, – above all, would we place in the hand of every right-thinking man, a whip to scourge from society the authors of such vile blasphemies as on Sunday night, above the cries of the dead and the dying, and louder than the wails of misery from the maimed and suffering, resounded from the mouth of Mr Spurgeon in the Music Hall of the Surrey Gardens."

A fund was raised to help the poor sufferers, and to avoid all fear of further panic the preacher resolved to hold the service in the morning, though that part of the day is least favourable to large congregations. The multitude came, however, and continued still to come for three good years. All classes came, both high and low. We have before us a list of the nobility who attended the Music Hall, but as we never felt any great elation at their attendance, or cared to have their presence blazoned abroad, we will not insert the names. It was a far greater joy to us that hundreds came who were led to seek the Lord, and to find eternal life in him.

A famous letter, signed *Habitans in Sicco*, and dated from Broad Phylactery, Westminster, appeared at this period in the *Times,* and as it was known to be written by an eminent scholar, it produced a very favourable impression. Part of the letter ran as follows: –

"'I want to hear Spurgeon; let us go.' Now, I am supposed to be a high churchman, so I answered, 'What! go and hear a Calvinist – a Baptist! – a man who ought to be ashamed of himself for being so near the Church, and yet not within its pale?' 'Never mind; come and hear him.' Well, we went yesterday morning to the Music Hall, in the Surrey Gardens ... Fancy a congregation consisting of 10,000 souls, streaming into the Hall, mounting the galleries, humming, buzzing, and swarming – a mighty hive of bees – eager to secure at first the best places, and, at last, any place at all. After waiting more than half an hour – for if you wish to have a seat you must be there at least that space of time in advance – Mr Spurgeon ascended his tribune. To the hum, and rush, and trampling of men, succeeded a low, concentrated thrill and murmur of devotion, which seemed to run at once, like an electric current, through the breast of everyone present; and by this magnetic chain, the preacher held us fast bound for about two hours. It is not my purpose to give a summary of his discourse. It is enough to say of his voice, that its power and volume are sufficient to reach everyone in that vast assembly; of his language, that it is neither high-flown nor homely; of his style, that it is at times familiar, at times declamatory, but always happy, and often eloquent; of his doctrine, that neither the Calvinist nor the Baptist appears in the forefront of the battle which is waged by Mr Spurgeon with relentless animosity, and with gospel weapons, against irreligion, cant, hypocrisy, pride, and those secret bosom sins which so easily beset a man in daily life; and to sum up all in a word, it is enough to say of the man himself that he impresses you with a perfect conviction of his sincerity.

"But I have not written so much about my children's want of spiritual food when they listened to the mumbling of the Archbishop of _____, and my own banquet at the Surrey Gardens, without a desire to draw a practical conclusion from these two stories, and to point them by a moral. Here is a man not more Calvinistic than many an incumbent of the Established Church, who 'humbles and mumbles,' as old Latimer says, over his liturgy and text – here is a man who says the complete immersion, or something of the kind, of adults is necessary to baptism. These are his faults of doctrine; but if I were the examining chaplain of the Archbishop of _____, I would say, 'May it please your grace, here is a man able to preach eloquently, able to fill the largest church in England with his voice, and what is more to the purpose, with people. And may it please your grace, here are two churches in the metropolis, St Paul's and Westminster Abbey. What does your grace think of inviting Mr Spurgeon, this heretical Calvinist and Baptist, who is able to draw 10,000 souls after him, just to try his voice, some Sunday morning, in the nave of either of those churches?'"

On October 7th, 1857, the day of National Humiliation for the Indian Mutiny, Mr Spurgeon preached in the centre transept of the Crystal Palace to more than 23,000 people, and the sum of £686 was paid over to the National Fund.

Meanwhile the collection of funds for a new building went on, and in January, 1858, the money in hand was £6100; by January, 1859, it was £9,639, and £5,000 of it was set aside to pay for the ground near the Elephant and Castle. We went plodding on, the pastor collecting personally, or by his sermons, very much of the money, travelling far and wide to do so; Scottish friends especially helping; until in January, 1860, after the first stone had been laid, £16,868 was in hand, or more than half of the sum required, so that the land had been paid for, and instalments paid to the builder as required. The first stone of the Metropolitan Tabernacle was laid with great rejoicings, August 16th, 1859, by Sir Morton Peto; but as a report of the whole proceedings can be procured of our publishers we will say but little here. We feel constrained, however, to mention the singular providence which placed Mr Spicer and other friends upon the Court of the Fishmongers' Company, so as to secure the land; next, the fact that the company was able to sell the freehold; and, next, that the late Mr William Joynson, of Mary Cray, deposited the amount to pay for an Act of Parliament to enable the company to sell in case it had turned out that they had not the legal power to do so. Singularly happy also was the circumstance that a gentleman in Bristol, who had never heard the pastor, nevertheless gave no less a sum than £5,000 towards the building. Eternity alone can reveal all the generous feeling and self-denying liberality shown by Christian people in connection with this enterprise – to us at any rate so gigantic at the time that apart from divine aid we could never have carried it through. One of the chief of our mercies was the fact that our beloved brother, William Higgs, was our builder, and treated us with unbounded liberality throughout the whole affair. He is now a worthy deacon of our church.

In December, 1859, we left the Surrey Music Hall. We paid the company a large sum for our morning service, and this was the only amount out of which a dividend was paid. They proposed to open the gardens for amusement on the Lord's Day evening, and we threatened to give up our tenancy if they did so. This prevented the evil for some time, but at length the baser sort prevailed, and under the notion that Sunday "pleasure" would prove remunerative, they advertised that the gardens would be opened on the Sabbath: we, therefore, felt bound in honour to leave the place, and we did so. After a while a fire almost destroyed the building, and the relics were for years turned into a hospital. We commenced on December 18th, 1859, our third and longest sojourn at Exeter Hall, which ended on March 1st, 1861. A few of our remarks upon leaving that place may fitly be quoted here.

"In the providence of God we, as a church and people, have had to wander often. This is our third sojourn within these walls. It is now about to close. We have had at all times and seasons a compulsion for moving: sometimes a compulsion of conscience, at other times a compulsion of pleasure, as on this occasion. I am sure that when we first went to the Surrey Music Hall, God went with us. Satan went too, but he fled before us. That frightful calamity, the impression of which can never be erased from my mind, turned out in the providence of God to be one of the most wonderful means of turning public attention to special services, and I do not doubt that – fearful catastrophe though it was – it has been the mother of multitudes of blessings. The Christian world noted the example; and saw its after-success; they followed it; and to this day, in the theatre and in the cathedral, the Word of Christ is preached where it was never preached before. In each of our movings we have had reason to see the hand of God, and here particularly; for many residents in the West End have in this place come to listen to the Word, who probably might not have taken a journey beyond the river. Here God's grace has broken hard hearts; here have souls been renewed, and wanderers reclaimed. 'Give unto the Lord, O ye mighty, give unto the Lord glory and strength; give unto the Lord the glory due unto his name.' And now we journey to the house which God has in so special a manner given to us, and this day would I pray as Moses did, 'Rise up, Lord, and let thine enemies be scattered, and let them that hate thee flee before thee.'"

In 1859, the church for the first time appointed Elders to aid the Pastor in the *spiritual* concerns of the church. This arrangement has been of vital importance and has met a manifest necessity. Of honoured men who have filled this office we could mention many names, but it would extend this history beyond our limits.

In February 1860, the Pastor visited Paris, preaching in the Eglise de l'Oratoire, and in the American Chapel, to crowded houses. At this time M. Provost Paradol wrote an enthusiastic critique, which from a Catholic was the more remarkable. We have, however, no space for it, nor for more than an allusion to sermons preached in June of this year in Geneva, in the Cathedral from the pulpit of John Calvin, and in the church of M. D'Aubigné.

Under date January 6th, 1861, there stands in our records the following solemn declaration, signed by the pastor and leading friends: – "This church needs rather more than £4,000 to enable it to open the New Tabernacle free of all debt. It humbly asks this temporal mercy of God, and believes that for Jesus' sake the prayer will be heard and the boon bestowed. As witness our hands."

Now let the reader mark that, on May 6th of the same year, the Pastor and many friends also signed their names to another testimony, which is worded as follows: "We, the undersigned members of the church lately worshipping in New Park Street Chapel, but now assembling in the Metropolitan Tabernacle, Newington, desire with overflowing hearts to make known and record the loving-kindness of our faithful God. We asked in faith, but our Lord has exceeded our desires, for not only was the whole sum given us, but far sooner than we had looked for it. Truly the Lord is good and worthy to be praised. We are ashamed of ourselves that we have ever doubted him, and we pray that, as a church, and as individuals, we may be enabled to trust in the Lord at all times with confidence, so that in quietness we may possess our souls. To Father, Son, and Holy Ghost we offer praise and thanksgiving, and we set to our seal that God is true."

After about a month of Opening Services of which a full account can be had of our publishers, we began regular work at the Tabernacle in May 1861, the whole building being *free of debt*, and the accounts showing that £31,332 4s. 10d. had been received, and the same amount expended. Truly we serve a gracious God.

The Tabernacle is 146 feet long, 81 feet broad, and 62 feet high. There are some 5,500 sittings of all kinds. There is room for 6,000 persons without excessive crowding; and we have also a lecture-hall holding about 900, a schoolroom for 1,000 children, six class-rooms, kitchen, lavatory, and retiring rooms below stairs. We have a ladies' room for working meetings, young men's class-room, and Secretary's room on the ground floor; three vestries, for pastor, deacons, and elders on the first floor, and three store-rooms on the second floor. The accommodation is all too little for the work to be carried on, and we are glad to use the rooms at the almshouses and the college.

During the month of January, 1863, the Pastor preached in most of the large towns of Holland, and had a lengthened interview with the Queen of the Netherlands. The sermons are widely circulated in the Dutch language.

In the month of June, 1864, a sermon was preached by C H S in the Metropolitan Tabernacle which raised a widespread controversy, upon the important subject of Baptismal Regeneration. Rectors, and curates, and deans, and canons, rose in the fulness of their indignation, and fulminated pamphlets, which were met with replies of equal warmth. The sermon itself has reached a circulation of 200,000, and remains as our earnest protest against the unnatural use of language by the clergy, and as a proof positive that the Book of Common Prayer contains words which are calculated to teach the most deadly error. The vituperation which followed upon this discourse has been cheerfully endured for the truth's sake, until at this moment some of our fiercest opponents are our friends, and hundreds who were led to look into the matter for the first time are now among our firmest adherents. When the time comes, some curious incidents connected with this conflict may be narrated, but not now.

Many interesting events have occurred since then, but we have not space to record them. In May, 1867, while the Tabernacle was repaired, we occupied the Agricultural Hall for five Sabbaths, and had it crowded every morning with not less than 20,000 persons, and what is better, the Holy Spirit put life and power into the Word.

In October, 1867, the Pastor having for several years been laid aside at intervals by painful illness, and it having been stated by eminent physicians that this was due to the over-straining of his mental powers, the deacons and elders, after consulting together, recommended the church to request Mr J A SPURGEON to become co-pastor with his brother, to relieve him of much of the pastoral work. This happy arrangement was carried out January 9, 1868, and has been a great comfort to the senior pastor, both in church and college work. Mr James Spurgeon is now also the pastor of a large and growing church in Croydon, for which he has erected a noble chapel,

James A Spurgeon

where he is able to exercise his ministry on the Lord's Day; his help being mainly required at the Tabernacle upon week-days, and in the general oversight of the church. No more efficient or sympathetic helper could possibly have been found.

Here we may claim space to notice how much the church of late years has been indebted to some of her departed workers; for instance, Deacon Thomas Cook, who superintended the work of collecting funds for the New Tabernacle; to Elder Dransfield, one of the happiest and most useful Christians in the world; and to Mrs Bartlett, whose loss we cannot cease to deplore, for she not only led hundreds of young women to Jesus, but was also a pastor and mother to them. Among those who are yet living, there are some of the best and most gracious of men and women, but it would be invidious to name some where so many are doing their best. Yet, even at the risk of this evil, we must mention our Deacon William Olney, whose illness is a calamity to us all, and Deacon W C Murrell, who for many years has borne all the buffetings of the crowd at the doors and by the sacrifice of his own personal comfort has enabled us to worship in peace and quietness.

To us the most noteworthy fact has been the increase of our membership. Of this we subjoin a table.

Close of Year	Membership	Gross increase	Clear increase
1854	313		
1855	595	282	282
1856	860	279	265
1857	1046	216	186
1858	1183	231	137
1859	1332	217	149
1860	1494	217	162
1861	1875	439	381
1862	2227	463	352
1863	2555	427	328
1864	2937	486	382
1865	3293	497	356
1866	3458	447	165
1867	3682	413	224
1868	3888	452	206
1869	4047	451	159

1870	4165	409	118
1871	4165	312	–
1872	4473	571	308
1873	4503	359	30
1874	4681	509	178
1875	4813	510	132

From this it will be seen how steadily the process of addition to the church has gone on even in those years in which the *clear* increase has been small. Had we lost none, we should now number 8,500. Emigrations and removals to other churches take from us so large a number that it has in some years needed three persons to be added in the gross to secure a permanent increase of one. Nor does this at all distress us; it is well that it should be so. If the converts all remained in our church, the Tabernacle would not hold them, and there would certainly be no room for the unconverted to come and hear; but now we pass them on to other churches with pleasure, believing that they will be a salt in the earth, and rejoicing that others are being drawn by the Spirit to fill their places. We can hardly expect to increase beyond 5,000 as we have not sufficient seat room for more than that number.

Out of these converts a very large number have become ministers, colporteurs, and City missionaries, and of late the missionary spirit has also been developed, so that quite a number of our friends have gone forth among the heathen, to our great joy and rejoicing.

At this date (March, 1876) all is proceeding with regularity and life under the divine smile. Our Deacons number nine, and our Elders thirty-one. Mr J T Dunn aids us in visitation and discipline, and Mr Charlesworth, the Head Master of the Orphanage, is also a great assistance to us in conducting Bible Classes and public services.

The *Sermons*, published weekly, have now reached No. 1,284, and the *Sword and Trowel* is in the 12th volume; the circulation of both being well sustained.

We have almost completed the 22nd year of our pastorate, and though we long to see greater things, yet we magnify the name of the Lord as we hear the watchman cry, "ALL IS WELL."

9
"Father" Olney

THERE were several worthy men in the deacon's office when we first came to London; but out of them all, our friend, our counsellor, our right hand, was THOMAS OLNEY. No minister ever had a better deacon, nor church a better servant. He died in 1869, and at this moment we miss him still, and so do hundreds of the Lord's poor, to whom he was an incarnate providence. In his house we first enjoyed hospitality when we came to New Park Street, he sat in the pulpit with us at the Surrey Gardens in order to communicate our wishes to those who kept order, and he so frequently travelled with us that some jocose friend called him our "dry-nurse." He was our model deacon, and take him for all in all we ne'er shall look upon his like again.

We know something about deacons, and all we know is to their honour. Those of our first village ministry were the excellent of the earth, in whom we took great delight. Since our sojourn in London we have seen the last of a former race of deacons; fine, gentlemanly men, rather stiff and unmanageable, not quite to our mind, but respectable, prudent grandees of Dissent, in semi-clerical dress, with white cravats. Our present staff of deacons consists of peculiarly lovable, active, energetic, warm-hearted, generous men; but as we may hope to live with them for another quarter of a century, we will only say of them that we love them heartily and find them true yoke-fellows.

Thomas Olney, Snr, has left us another Thomas Olney, Treasurer, in the person of his son, and a William Olney, Deacon, who is greatly beloved by us all, and is the daily subject of our earnest prayers that he may be restored to health and spared to us for many years to come. There is also another generation of Olneys springing up, one of whom has already distinguished himself as a leading worker among us.

Thomas Olney was born at Tring, November 10th, 1790. His father, Mr Daniel Olney, was for many years a deacon of the Baptist church in that town. Thomas was sent to London, and apprenticed in the City to a wholesale mercer. From his first entrance into London he attended the ministry of Dr Rippon, at Carter Lane. Here the Lord graciously met with him and saved his soul. He was proposed as a candidate for church fellowship, December, 1809, and remained for sixty years a member of the church. He was accustomed, even in their earliest years, to take his children to Carter Lane Chapel, having a little chair fixed on the pew-seat for the youngest.

In 1817, an early Sabbath-morning lecture was commenced in Carter Lane Chapel. To be at the service by half-past six o'clock, to collect the necessary funds, and to welcome the various ministers, was Mr Olney's great delight.

His closest friendships were formed within the circle of the church. Not only did he say of the church, "Thy God shall be my God," but also, "Thy people shall be my people."

In 1829 Carter Lane Chapel became the property of the City, and was pulled down; Dr Rippon became old and feeble; the love of many waxed cold, and they left the church in its hour of peril. Not so Thomas Olney: he remained manfully with the church. He was appointed a trustee for the chapel in New Park Street, opened in 1833. His much-loved pastor, Dr Rippon, expired in his presence, it might as properly be said in his arms. It was his privilege for some

Thomas Olney

months, by his care and kindness, to cheer the last days of his highly-esteemed friend, towards whose memory he cherished until his last days a most tender affection.

During all the time of erecting the new chapel in New Park Street, Mr Olney may be said to have "favoured the very dust of Zion." From foundation to top-stone he watched its progress with interest and prayer. Prosperity was given under the ministry of Mr James Smith, and it was Mr Olney's happiness to see all his four sons baptised and united to the church. In 1838, he was, together with his friend Mr Winsor, chosen deacon of the church. He faithfully served in that office thirty-one years. *He was ever remarkable for his early and constant attendance at the prayer meeting and other week-day services.* He loved the habitation of God's house.

God had other mercies in store for him. His beloved Zion was to rise and shine. By the providence of God, Deacon Olney had his attention directed by his old friend, the late Mr G Gould, of Loughton, to the present Pastor, under whom, through the divine blessing, the church has grown and multiplied.

A new and far larger building was needed; a meeting in Mr Olney's house commenced the undertaking, and the work after much pains and prayer was accomplished. In 1855, "Father Olney," as he was playfully styled by Pastor and Deacons, was chosen treasurer of the church, and by the help of his sons fulfilled the office, together with those of Deacon and Elder, until his death.

He was treasurer fourteen years. "Of his love and devotion to both the pastor and the church we all are witnesses." His greatest pride, we might almost use that word, was the work of God at the Tabernacle. He gloried and rejoiced in all that concerned the church. He loved college, orphanage, and almshouses, and helped them all to the extent of his ability. His fellow officers in the deaconship shared his esteem and love. And now that he has changed earthly for heavenly service and joy, may his memory and example stir us all to copy and follow him as far as he followed Christ.

Our departed friend had a childlike faith and a manly constancy. To believe in Jesus and to work for him were the very life of his new and better nature. He was eminently a Baptist, but he was also a lover of all good men. The poor, and especially the poor of the church, always found in him sincere sympathy and help. His name will be had in lasting remembrance.

10
Internal Condition in 1869

THE *Sword and Trowel* for February, 1869, contains a paper which conveys a better idea of the condition and work of our church at that period than anything fresh which we are able to write. In almost all respects it accurately describes the present (1876), but as that part which relates to *the work* of the church is much changed, we have omitted it.

Discipline of the Church at the Metropolitan Tabernacle
By J A Spurgeon

The *subject* of this paper is the discipline of the church at the Metropolitan Tabernacle. This particular example has been selected because with it the writer is more familiar than with any other. It is, moreover, the discipline of one of our oldest churches, and not the least successful of them, and it has been thought that there are elements of peculiar interest connected with it which it would be useful to enumerate.

We are anxious to disclaim, at the outset, any pretensions to perfection in our methods of action – we have found them to work best for ourselves hitherto, but we are always anxious to find out a more excellent way. Our plans have been the outgrowth of necessity, not of theory; they were not sketched on paper and then carried out as an experiment, but the circumstances of the church drove us to our present methods, and we hope we have seen a line of scriptural precedent justifying our obedience to providential indications. We should regret exceedingly if for a moment it were supposed that we would recommend absolute uniformity in the methods of discipline adopted by churches; but to our minds thus much is clear, that the congregational churches, both Baptist and Paedobaptist, have gone as far in the direction of diversity as possible, and weakness rather than strength has been the result. That no room should be left for the different peculiarities of pastor and people, but all be bound to one undeviating standard of action, would be to cramp, and not to benefit; but, on the other hand, that so few points of agreement should be accepted as a common basis of action, sustaining a sense of confidence in each other's discipline, is little short of a calamity. Mutual confidence arising from known adequate, though it may be at times dissimilar, courses of action, leading up to one result, must be a source of blessing to any denomination; and at present we frankly admit, as the result of a somewhat wide observation of the methods of receiving, and the all but uniform want of method in removing, names from our church rolls, we have but small faith in ecclesiastical statistics, and what is worse, a limited confidence in letters of commendation from our churches. That we may all find room for improvement is undoubted, and that we may at once make the discovery and act upon it, is the object and prayer of the writer of this paper.

We remark at once that at the Tabernacle *we have no written code of laws but the Book of Inspiration*, and we unhesitatingly assert that all such printed rules as some have desired, and others adopted, are only fetters at the best of times, and snares and traps in periods of dispute and difficulty. We have faith in sanctified common sense, resulting from an application to the source of all wisdom by prayer and reading the Scriptures. If churches would only act with the prudence of assemblies of mercantile men, much evil would be averted, and more good secured. Acting in things temporal after a truly business principle, and in things spiritual as God's Word and Spirit dictate, no formal system of rules, in our opinion, will ever be required. Certain recognised courses of procedure, from which, without cause assigned, no deviation shall be made, are certainly necessary for mutual co-operation and peace in any church; but for emergencies, special action should be adopted to suit the exigencies of the case, and no rules or traditions must forbid the course which wisdom suggests, even though it should be contrary to all the precedents of the previous history of the church. A general understanding of leading principles, and an elastic interpretation of them as cases may require, will be all the rule outside of the Scripture required in churches where confidence abounds between pastors, officers, and members; if this be wanting, no rules, human or divine, can make them work harmoniously together. We must have faith in each other's intentions and integrity, or we shall loosen the pins of church action, and all will lapse into confusion and conflict.

Church Officers

Principles of action however clear, and methods of procedure however established by custom, will be of little avail if they be not sustained by a vigorous executive. Amongst the officers of the church, foremost stands *the Pastor*, who, though its servant, is so to rule, guide, and discipline it as God shall help and direct by his Holy Spirit. In connection with the church at the Tabernacle, two such officers are now labouring. It is a trite remark that if two men ride a horse one must sit behind, and he who is in the front must hold the reins and drive. Co-pastorships have been sources of discomfort or blessing as this principle has been understood. Wherever it may have been disregarded, it is not (by the grace of God) likely to be so in the case in hand. Where one of the two brothers has been so instrumental in creating the necessity for additional help, from the very fulness of blessing resulting from his labours; and is, moreover, so superior in talent, influence, and power, [1] it is a privilege to follow in the order of nature and birth which God, from the first, had evidently designed.

The discipline of the church thus emanates from a common centre, acting through recognised division of labour. All meetings and institutions are subject to the influence, and when required, to the action of the Pastorate. It would be, at least, unseemly to have a hydra-headed band of Christians. Sunday School, college, orphanage, almshouses, psalmody, are all under the supervision of a common headship, so as to prevent almost inevitable confusion, if not conflict, as the result of divided action. The leader of the church should surely lead the church's work. Strife without measure has arisen from rival authorities disputing about the boundaries of their little empires. The spirit of peace has kept us from this evil, but a judicious arrangement has been helpful in producing the result. There are still Diotrephes in the present age – men loving to have the pre-eminence – but it is the duty of the minister to magnify his office, and rule even these, which is best done, not by assertions of power or complaints of want of influence, but by possessing such personal weight of piety and prudence, zeal, godliness, gentleness, and forbearance as will inevitably place him in the front in course of time. In the long run, the measure of any man's power and influence is the measure in which he deserves to possess them; and no man is entitled to expect any more. It is quite certain that no efforts to assert official dignity, when sound judgment and weight of character are wanting, will ever result in anything short of failure and contempt. We have known some whose claims for deference and respect were in the inverse ratio to their deserts; and the only outgrowth of their priestlyism was to ruin and break up every church they attempted to guide and control. How much we need the wisdom of the serpent with the harmlessness of the dove! How gently, as a nurse among her children, should the pastor behave himself! With what unassuming brotherly love, and paternal wisdom, should he hold intercourse with his people! True pastors must be both made and born; and day by day must they be sustained, or their office will be a shame to themselves and a burden to their flocks. From this may the Lord keep his servants evermore.

Deacons and Elders – After the Pastor, and labouring by his side, we need brethren qualified of God to be helpers of our joy. In this church, two offices distinct in main points, though often coincident in others, are recognised, and, as we think, with both Scripture and common sense upon our side. It may and does often happen that the man of judgement, prudent in counsel, and skilled in money matters, is not gifted with speech so as to lead devotional exercises in the church or prayer meetings, or beside the bed of sickness, or in the house of mourning. A good man for things temporal, in dealing with worldly matters, may not be an elder apt to teach and to exhort. On the other hand, a man may have all the qualifications of an elder, but be lacking in such abilities as are required for the serving of tables, the disposing of finances, and the securing of needed funds for the church.

Our *Deacons*, nine in number, are elected by the church at the suggestion of the Pastor after consultation with the previously elected deacons. It is open to any member to nominate whom he pleases at such an election, but in no case has the recommendation of the Pastor and Deacons been dissented from, for the brethren nominated were in every way called and qualified of the Lord. They are chosen for life: this having been the usual custom in such cases; and there being no strong reason for a change in the rule. Their duties are to care for the ministry, and help the poor of the church, to regulate the finances and take charge of the church's property, seeing to the order and comfort of all worshipping in the place. The work is divided so as to secure the services of all, and prevent the neglect of anything through uncertainty as to the person responsible for its performance. One honoured brother is generally treasurer, and has been so for many years – long may he be spared to us; another takes all outdoor work, repairs, keeping the gates, appointing door-keepers, and so on; a third attends to the relief of the poor, and a fourth as a good steward, sees to the arrangement and provision of the Lord's Table; thus with a common council we have separate duties. At every remembrance of these brethren we thank God. Some ministers have found their trials in their deacons; it is but right to say that we find in them our greatest comfort, and we earnestly desire that every church should share in an equal blessing.

Elders – Our eldership, now sustained by twenty-six brethren, is a source of much blessing to our church. Without the efficient and self-denying labours of the Elders we should never be able to supervise our huge church, containing at the close of the year 1868, 3,860 members, and from which, under the present pastor, about an equal number have gone to the church triumphant, or to other parts of the church militant.

The Elders are re-elected annually, but usually continue for life in their office; fresh Elders are proposed by the Pastor to the already elected Elders, and after some time has been given for thought, the subject of the propriety of their election is discussed at an Elders' meeting, and if recommended with general unanimity, the names are then laid before the church by the Pastor, and, after opportunity given for the expression of opinion, the vote of the church is taken. We offer no opinion here as to other methods of electing church officers, but we will add that no other plan commends itself so much to our judgment; no other plan is so safe for our church, or so likely to procure good officers; no other plan is so helpful to the Pastor, who is most concerned in the choice, having to work with those selected; and no other plan as we can see will enable him so faithfully to discharge his office of guide and shepherd, in one of the most critical periods of the church's history. Timidity here is a crime, and the affectation of modesty in not wishing to influence the church is to our mind dereliction of duty. A church possessed of unlimited liberty of action, needs, for the sake of its junior and less instructed members, to be directed in its choice of officers – the best men to do it are the pastor and officers already tried and proved, and the fear of giving offence seems to us but the fear of man, which bringeth a snare.

To the Elders is committed the spiritual oversight of the church, and such of its concerns as are not assigned to the Deacons nor belong to the preacher. The seeing of enquirers, the visiting of candidates for church membership, the seeking out of absentees, the caring for the sick and troubled, the conducting of prayer meetings, catechumen and Bible-classes for the young men – these and other needed offices our brethren the Elders discharge for the church. One Elder is maintained by the church for the especial purpose of visiting our sick poor, and looking after the church roll, that this may be done regularly and efficiently. As a whole we cheerfully bear our testimony to the beneficial working of the system of deaconate and eldership as distinct offices. Both works are in a few cases performed by the same person, but the existence of the two bodies of men is in a thousand ways a great assistance to good government.

Church Membership

All persons anxious to join our church are requested to apply personally upon any Wednesday evening, between six and nine o'clock, to the elders, two or more of whom attend in rotation every week for the purpose of seeing enquirers. When satisfied, the case is entered by the elder in one of a set of books provided for the purpose, and a card is given bearing a corresponding number to the page of the book in which particulars of the candidate's experience are recorded. Once a month, or more often when required, the junior pastor appoints a day to see the persons thus approved of by the elders. If the pastor is satisfied, he nominates an elder or church member as visitor, and at the next church meeting asks the church to send him to enquire as to the moral character and repute of the candidate. If the visitor is satisfied, he requests the candidate to attend with him at the following or next convenient church meeting, to come before the church and reply to such questions as may be put from the chair, mainly with a view to elicit expressions of his trust in the Lord Jesus, and hope of salvation through his blood, and any such facts of his spiritual history as may convince the church of the genuineness of the case. We have found this a means of grace and a rich blessing. None need apprehend that modesty is outraged, or timidity appalled by the test thus applied. We have never yet found it tend to keep members out of our midst, while we have known it of service in detecting a mistake or satisfying a doubt previously entertained. We deny that it keeps away any worth having. Surely if their Christianity cannot stand before a body of believers, and speak amongst loving, sympathising hearts, it is as well to ask if it be the cross-bearing public confessing faith of the Bible? This is no matter of flesh and blood, but of faith and grace, and we should be sorry to give place to the weakness and shrinking of the flesh, so as to insult the omnipotence of grace, by deeming it unable to endure so much as the telling in the gates of Zion what great things God has done for the soul. Of course, the system may be, and has been, abused, but we decline to recognise any argument drawn from the abuse of what we use lawfully. After the statement before the church, the candidate withdraws, the visitor gives in his report, and the vote of the church is taken; when the candidate has professed his faith by immersion, which is administered by the junior pastor, after a week-day service, he is received by the pastor at the first monthly communion, when the right hand of fellowship is given to him in the name of the church, and his name is entered on the roll of members. A communion card is furnished, divided by perforation into twelve numbered parts, one of which is to be delivered every month at the communion, which is held every Lord's Day; the tickets are checked upon the register, and thus show the attendance of each member at the communion. If a member is absent more than three months without any known cause, the elder in whose district he resides is requested to visit him, and send in a report on a printed form which is given him; or if the residence be distant, a letter is written, a record of such visit or letter being retained. When a case for discipline presents itself, it is brought before the elders, who appoint one of their number to visit and report; if the matter demands action beyond caution and advice, we lay it before the church, and recommend the course of procedure to be adopted, whether censure or excommunication.

In dealing with such as are members of other churches, we have been by sad experience compelled to exercise more caution than at first seemed needful. The plan we adopt is to have the person seen by an elder, who enters particulars in the transfer book. If there appears to be any difficulty, an interview is arranged with one of the pastors who investigates the case on its own merits, as, alas! he has discovered that membership with some churches is not always a guarantee even of morality. Some churches retain a name upon their books for years after the person has ceased to commune; and frequently when he has passed away from all knowledge of, or connection with the church, it will nevertheless grant a transfer as if all were satisfactory. We record this with mingled shame and sorrow. When the individual has thus given evidence of fitness, so far as we can judge, a dismissal is applied for in the usual way, and the reply is laid before the church, any information necessary is added, and the vote of the church taken.

When, in the order of God's providence, any of our number are removed from us, and are not able to attend, a certificate is given for three, six, or twelve months, which must then be renewed, and a report of the reason for renewal given, or the membership will lapse, unless in special cases. We much prefer commending our brethren to the fellowship of other churches, where they may be of service, than to have them maintain a merely nominal connection with us. We have thus sent from us 166 in the course of last year, we hope to the strengthening of the churches and the spread of the truth.

On receipt of application from any church for the transfer of a member, a letter is read to the church, with the detailed account from our books, giving a brief but complete history of the case, when and how received, the attendance of the person while a member with us, and reasons for seeking removal. The church is then advised to authorise the usual letter of dismission to be sent.

In all our business the aim is to have everything done openly and above-board, so that no one may complain of the existence of a clique, or the suppression of the true state of affairs. We occasionally ask the unquestioning confidence of the church in its officers in cases delicate and undesirable to be published, but otherwise we consult the church in everything, and report progress as often as possible in all matters still pending and unsettled. Nothing, we are persuaded, is so sure to create suspicion and destroy confidence as attempts at secret diplomacy, or mere official action.

When details of cases under discipline are kept from the church, the fact is openly stated, and leave asked for the maintenance of such public reticence; while any member is informed that, if dissatisfied, the pastor will give him the reasons why the elders have advised the removal of the offender, and their motive in not giving details of the sin. When it would be for the injury of good morals, or expose the pastor to a suit-at-law, the officers ask the confidence of the church, and request it to adopt their verdict in the case without hearing detailed information; this is cheerfully accorded in every case, and much evil is thus averted.

All money matters are audited by unofficial brethren selected by the church, and the accounts read and books produced at the annual church meeting, when all the members endeavour to be present.

All minutes of church meetings, deacons' and elders' courts, are entered, and confirmed at the following meeting, Unless notice is previously given, no business, as a rule, is entertained in the church meeting, except it emanates from the chair, or is sent up from an elders' session; though this custom is departed from if any manifest benefit is to be derived from so doing, and no one challenges the motion as irregular.

In conclusion, we feel bound to acknowledge that our dependence for prosperity and peace is solely upon the God who commands the dew of his grace to descend upon his church. All our springs are in him; no under-shepherd's care, not the best built and guarded fold, can ever keep out the wolf in sheep's clothing, nor the enemy so watchful and relentless, who goeth about as a roaring lion, seeking whom he may devour. Our help cometh from the Lord who made heaven and earth. The discipline of the closet and the prayer meeting, of close fellowship with God in secret, will bring the reward openly. Nothing in the shape of rules or customs, no, not even the devoted services of apostles themselves, can compensate for low-toned piety on the part of the members. Whence come wars and fightings – is it not because many professors are still carnal, and walk not after the Spirit? Drawing nearer and nearer to the centre and source of all grace and blessing will inevitably result in our being "one" to the glory of God the Father. We must raise our standard of individual and personal piety, and to that extent we shall destroy elements of evil. If thorns can spring up and choke the good seed, the same law may, if rightly turned upon the foe, destroy roots of bitterness which, springing up, would trouble us, by occupying the ground with the "fruits of the Spirit, which are love, joy, peace, long-suffering, gentleness, goodness, faith, meekness, temperance: against such there is no law."

"Now unto him that is able to keep you from falling, and to present you faultless before the presence of his glory with exceeding joy, to the only wise God our Saviour, be glory and majesty, dominion and power, both now and for ever. Amen."

11

The Almshouses

WHEN we built the Tabernacle we looked upon New Park Street Chapel as a property which we would endeavour to retain for the Baptist denomination, and we desired if possible to make it the abode of another church. For some years preaching was carried on, a brother supported, and considerable expenses incurred, but it was clear that a self-sustaining interest was not to be gathered in the neighbourhood. Mr J Collins, now of Penge, worked very hard, and enjoyed much of the divine blessing, but those who were converted under him had a pardonable tendency to gravitate towards the mother church at the Tabernacle, and it became evident beyond all question that it was useless for us to retain so large a building in such a situation and so near our own. The property consisted of the chapel, schools, and almsrooms, and it was agreed, and arranged with the Charity Commissioners, that it should be sold, and the proceeds used for new schools and almsrooms, The inmates of the rooms greatly rejoiced at the prospect of coming nearer the Tabernacle and dwelling in a place where fresh air would be obtainable.

A site was purchased near the Elephant and Castle Railway Station – the buildings can be seen when the train stops at the station. The first stone was laid by Deacon Thomas Olney, May 6th, 1867, and the friends were requested to contribute about £1,000, which would be needed over and above the moneys in hand. This they did very promptly, but when the buildings were finished it was found that some £750 more would be needed to cover the extras which had been found necessary during the progress of the works. The pastor announced this fact one Sabbath morning, and also his determination that the institution should remain unoccupied until all was paid for; he also mentioned donations which would be given by himself, Deacons Olney and Higgs, and a friend, whereupon the congregation by collections that day made up the rest, so that no debt came upon the new establishment. This cardinal rule of avoiding all *debt* has been the means of great strength to us. People do not pay for things after they have them with half the readiness with which they subscribe to purchase them. Besides, the scriptural rule is, "Owe no man any thing."

There are seventeen almsrooms, two schoolrooms, and a classroom, which are occupied by 380 children on week-days, and there is also a house for the schoolmaster. At the present time a Sabbath school, special children's service, and an evangelistic meeting, with many other good works are in earnest operation at the place, including most of the usual machinery connected with places of worship.

Members of the church, being women above the age of sixty, and needing support, are eligible to become occupants of the rooms. They are generally chosen according to their number on the Church book and the urgency of the case. One of the inmates, Miss Fanny Gay, is in her 87th year, and has been a member of the church 69 years. She is an eminently devout, prudent, godly woman, and in past years rendered eminent service by her conversations with young women who needed instruction or comfort. It is a joy to provide a resting place for her and the other aged sisters.

The original endowments, after the payment of repairs, do not suffice wholly to provide for six inmates, and there are now seventeen; the support of the remaining eleven involves a heavy draught upon the communion fund of our church, which is already fully weighted with poor members. WE GREATLY NEED AT LEAST £5,000 TO ENDOW THE ALMHOUSES, AND PLACE THE INSTITUTION UPON A PROPER FOOTING. Already C H Spurgeon, Thomas Olney, and Thomas Greenwood have contributed £200 each towards the fund, and we earnestly trust that either by donations or legacies the rest of the £5,000 will be forthcoming. This would only provide five shillings per week for each poor woman, which is little enough. If more could be raised it would be so much the better for the pensioners. *The Pastors are anxious to see this matter put into proper order; they confess that the responsibility of having increased the number of rooms and almswomen rests mainly with them, and, therefore, they feel that their work is not done until at least five shillings per week shall have been provided for their poor sisters: if it could be double that amount they would be glad.* We wish to leave the Tabernacle in good working order when our work is done; but the present burden might prove far too heavy for our successors; indeed, they ought not to be saddled with it. In future years the church may find itself barely able to support its own expenses, and we do not think that we are justified in leaving it the legacy of so heavy a charge. Our present anxiety is to get the ship tight and trim, and this is one of the matters which is not in a satisfactory condition. Brethren, let us set it straight.

Our aged sisters are worthy of all that we can do for them, and their grateful faces often make our heart glad. We should like to see more alms-rooms, and we hope someone will build and endow a row for aged men. We have had a hint that this project is taking shape in the mind of a gener-ous friend: we hope he will carry it out in his own lifetime, rather than wait to have it done by a legacy.

Over the door of the girls' school is the following inscription: –

"THESE BUILDINGS ARE CONNECTED WITH
THE ANCIENT CHURCH NOW WORSHIPPING IN
THE METROPOLITAN TABERNACLE. SIX OF THE
ALMSHOUSES, TOGETHER WITH A SCHOOLROOM,
WERE BUILT AND ENDOWED UNDER THE PASTORATE
OF DR JOHN RIPPON, AT NEW PARK STREET,
SOUTHWARK. THE PRESENT STRUCTURES WERE
COMPLETED MARCH, 1868
C H AND J A SPURGEON, PASTORS."

In our engraving the schoolrooms are on the right, and the masters house is on the left; the almsrooms are in the houses between. The day schools are self-supporting, but there are no funds to pay the expenses of the other operations here carried on. The pastor generally has to pay for the gas, firing, and so on. from his own pocket, as the endowments are so scanty.

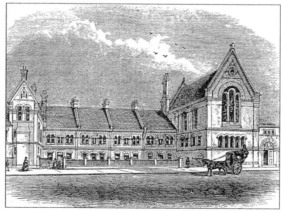

Metropolitan Tabernacle Almshouses

The investments now belonging to the almshouse trustees are, £2,950 reduced Consols, standing in different names; £400 Great Western Guaranteed 5 per cent Stock, presented by Mr T Olney and Mr C H Spurgeon; and £200 Buenos Aires Stock given by Mr Greenwood: they receive also £20 per annum as the rent of a small piece of ground and a hoarding for advertisements. Part of the principal endowment was left for repairs. We hope that in later editions of this history we shall be able to cancel this page and announce that the almshouses are amply provided for.

12
The Pastors' College

THE College was the first important institution commenced by the Pastor, and it still remains his firstborn and best beloved. To train ministers of the gospel is a most excellent work, and when the Holy Spirit blesses the effort, the result is of the utmost importance both to the church and to the world.

In the year 1870 we printed an account of the College, which we present to the reader as the best history we can furnish up to that date.

"The Pastors' College (commenced in 1856) has now entered on its fourteenth year, and during this long period has unceasingly been remembered of the God of heaven, to whom all engaged in it offer reverent thanksgiving. When it was commenced I had not even a remote idea of whereunto it would grow. There were springing up around me, as my own spiritual children, many earnest young men who felt an irresistible impulse to preach the gospel, and yet with half an eye it could be seen that their want of education would be a sad hindrance to them. It was not in my heart to bid them cease their preaching, and, had I done so, they would, in all probability, have ignored my recommendation. As it seemed that preach they would, though their attainments were very slender, no other course was open but to give them an opportunity to educate themselves for the work.

"The Holy Spirit very evidently had set his seal upon the work of one of them (Mr T W Medhurst, now of Landport) by conversions wrought under his open-air addresses: it seemed therefore to be a plain matter of duty to instruct this youthful Apollos still further, that he might be fitted for wider usefulness. No college at that time appeared to me to be suitable for the class of men that the providence and grace of God drew around me. They were mostly poor, and most of the colleges involved necessarily a considerable outlay to the student; for even where the education was free, books, clothes, and other incidental expenses required a considerable sum per annum. Moreover, it must be frankly admitted that my views of the gospel and of the mode of training preachers were and are somewhat peculiar. I may have been uncharitable in my judgement, but I thought the Calvinism of the theology usually taught to be very doubtful, and the fervour of the generality of the students to be far behind their

George Rogers

literary attainments. It seemed to me that preachers of the grand old truths of the gospel, ministers suitable for the masses, were more likely to be found in an institution where preaching and divinity would be the main objects, and not degrees and other insignia of human learning. I felt that without interfering with the laudable objects of other colleges, I could do good in my own way. These and other considerations led me to take a few tried young men, and to put them under some able minister that he might train them in the Scriptures, and in other knowledge helpful to the understanding and proclamation of the truth. This step appeared plain, but how the work was to be conducted and supported was the question – a question, be it added, solved almost before it occurred.

"Two friends, Mr Winsor and Mr W Olney, both deacons of the church, promised aid, which, with what I could give myself, enabled me to take one student, and I set about to find a tutor. In Mr George Rogers, then the pastor of the Independent Church, Albany Road, Camberwell, God sent us the very best man. He had been preparing for such work, and was anxiously waiting for it. This gentleman, who has remained during all this period our principal tutor, is a man of Puritanic stamp, deeply learned, orthodox in doctrine, judicious, witty, devout, earnest, liberal in spirit, and withal juvenile in heart to an extent most remarkable in one of his years. My connection with him has been one of uninterrupted comfort and delight. The most sincere affection exists between us, we are of one mind and of one heart, and what is equally important, he has in every case secured not merely the respect but the filial love of every student. Into this beloved minister's house the first students were introduced, and for a considerable period they were domiciled as members of his family.

"Encouraged by the readiness with which the young men found spheres of labour, and by their singular success in soul-winning, I enlarged the number, but the whole means of sustaining them came from my own purse. The large sale of my sermons in America, together with my dear wife's economy, enabled me to spend from £600 to £800 in a year in my own favourite work; but on a sudden, owing to my denunciations of the then existing slavery in the States, my entire resources from that 'brook Cherith' were dried up. I paid as large sums as I could from my own income, and resolved to spend all I had, and then take the cessation of my means as a voice from the Lord to stay the effort, as I am firmly persuaded that we ought under no pretence to go into debt. On one occasion I proposed the sale of my horse and carriage, although these were almost absolute necessaries to me on account of my continual journeys in preaching the Word. This my friend Mr Rogers would not hear of, and actually offered to be the loser rather than this should be done. Then it was that I told my difficulties to my people, and the *Weekly Offering* commenced, but the incomings from that source were so meagre as to be hardly worth calculating upon. I was brought to the last pound, when a letter came from a banker in the City, informing me that a lady, whose name I have never been able to discover, had deposited a sum of £200, to be used for the education of young men for the ministry. How did my heart leap for joy! I threw myself then and henceforth upon the bounteous care of the Lord, whom I desired with my whole heart to glorify by this effort. Some weeks after, another £100 came in from the same bank, as I was informed, from another hand. Soon after, Mr Phillips, a beloved deacon of the church at the Tabernacle, began to provide an annual supper for the friends of the College, at which considerable sums have from year to year been given. A dinner was also given by my liberal publishers, *Passmore and Alabaster*, to celebrate the publishing of my five hundredth weekly sermon, at which £500 was raised and presented to the funds. The College grew every month, and the number of students rapidly advanced from one to forty. Friends known and unknown, from far and near, were moved to give little or much to my work, and so the funds increased as the need enlarged. Then another earnest deacon of the church, Mr Murrell, espoused as his special work the weekly offering, and by the unanimous voice of the church under my care the College was adopted as its own child. Since that hour the weekly offering has been a steady source of income, until in the year 1869 the amount reached exactly £1,869.

"There have been during this period times of great trial of my faith; but after a season of straitness, never amounting to absolute want, the Lord has always interposed and sent me large sums (on one occasion £1,000) from unknown donors. When the Orphanage was thrust upon me, it did appear likely that this second work would drain the resources of the first, and it is very apparent that it does attract to itself some of the visible sources of supply, but my faith is firm that the Lord can as readily keep both works in action as one. My own present inability to do so much, by way of preaching abroad, occasions naturally the failure of another great source of income; and as my increasing labours at home will in all proba-bility diminish that stream in perpetuity, there is another trial of faith. Yet, if the Lord wills the work to be continued, he will send his servant a due portion of the gold and silver, which are all his own; and therefore as I wait upon him in prayer, the all-sufficient Provider will supply all my needs. About £5,000 is annually required for the College, and the same sum is needed for the Orphanage, but God will move his people to liberality, and we shall see greater things than these.

"While speaking of pecuniary matters, it may be well to add, that as many of the young men trained in the college have raised new congre-gations, and gathered fresh churches, another need has arisen – namely, money for building chapels. It is ever so in Christ's work, one link draws on another, one effort makes another needed. For chapel-building, the College funds could do but little, though they have freely been used to support men while they are collecting congregations; but the Lord found for me one of his stewards, who on the condition that his name remains unknown, has hitherto, as the Lord has prospered him, supplied very princely amounts for the erection of places of worship, of which more than forty have been built, or so greatly renovated and enlarged, as to be virtually new structures. Truly may it be said, 'What hath God wrought!'

"Pecuniary needs, however, have made up but a small part of our cares. Many have been my personal exercises in selecting the men. Candidates have always been plentiful, and the choice has been wide, but it is a seri-ous responsibility to reject any, and yet more to accept them for training. When mistakes have been made, a second burden has been laid upon me in the dismissal of those who appeared to be unfit. Even with the most careful management, and all the assistance of tutors and friends, no human foresight can secure that in every case a man shall be what we believed and hoped. A brother may be exceedingly useful as an occasional preacher, he may distinguish himself as a diligent student, he may succeed at first in the ministry, and yet, when trials of temper and character occur in the pastorate, he may be found wanting. We have had comparatively few causes for regret of this sort, but there have been some such, and these pierce us with many sorrows. I devoutly bless God that he has sent to the College some of the holiest, soundest, and most self-denying preachers I know, and I pray that he may continue to do so; but it would be more than a miracle if all should excel. While thus speaking of trials connected with the men themselves, it is due to our gracious God to bear testimony that these have been comparatively light, and are not worthy to be compared with the great joy which we experience in seeing no less than two hundred and seven brethren still serving the Lord according to their measure of gift, and all it is believed earnestly contending for the faith once delivered unto the saints; nor is the joy less in remembering that eleven have sweetly fallen asleep after having fought a good fight. At this hour some of our most flourishing Baptist churches are presided over by pastors trained in our College, and as years shall add ripeness of experience and stability of character, others will be found to stand in the front rank of the Lord's host.

"The young brethren are boarded generally in twos and threes, in the houses of our friends around the Tabernacle, for which the College pays a moderate weekly amount. The plan of separate lodging we believe to be far preferable to having all under one roof; for, by the latter mode, men are isolated from general family habits, and are too apt to fall into superabundant levity. The circumstances of the families who entertain our young friends are generally such that they are not elevated above the social position which in all probability they will have to occupy in future years, but are kept in connection with the struggles and conditions of everyday life.

"Devotional habits are cultivated to the utmost, and the students are urged to do as much evangelistic work as they can. The severe pressure put upon them to make the short term as useful as possible, leaves small leisure for such efforts, but this is in most instances faithfully economised. Although our usual period is two years, whenever it is thought right the term of study is lengthened to three or four years; indeed, there is no fixed rule, all arrangements being ordered by the circumstances and attainments of each individual.

"As before hinted, our numbers have greatly grown, and now range from eighty to one hundred. Very promising men, who are suddenly thrown in our way, are received at any time, and others who are selected from the main body of applicants come in at the commencement of terms. The church at the Tabernacle continues to furnish a large quota of men, and as these have usually been educated for two or more years in our Evening Classes, they are more advanced and better able to profit by our two years of study. We have no difficulty in finding spheres for men who are ready and fitted for them. There is no reason to believe that the supply of trained ministers is in advance of the demand. Even on the lowest ground of consideration, there is yet very much land to be possessed; and when men break up fresh soil, as ours are encouraged to do, the field is the world, and the prayer for more labourers is daily more urgent. If the Lord would but send us funds commensurate, there are hundreds of neighbourhoods needing the pure gospel, which we could by his grace change from deserts into gardens. *How far this is a call upon the reader let him judge as in the sight of God.* Shall there be the gifts and graces of the Spirit given to the church, and shall there not also be sufficient bestowed of the earthly treasure? How much owest thou unto my Lord?

"The College was for some little time aided by the zealous services of Mr W Cubitt, of Thrapstone, who died among us, enjoying our highest esteem. Mr Gracey, the classical tutor, a most able brother, is one of ourselves, and was in former years a student, though from possessing a solid education, he needed little instruction from us except in theology. In him we have one of the most efficient tutors living, a man fitted for any post requiring thorough scholarship, and aptness in communicating knowledge. Mr Fergusson, in the English elementary classes, does the first work upon the rough stones of the quarry, and we have heard from the men whom he has taught in the evening classes speeches and addresses which would have adorned any assembly, proving to demonstration his ability to cope with the difficulties of uncultured and ignorant minds. Mr Johnson, who zealously aids in the evening, is also a brother precisely suited to the post which he occupies. These *evening classes* afford an opportunity to Christian men engaged during the day to obtain an education for nothing during their leisure time, and very many avail themselves of the privilege. Nor must I forget to mention Mr Selway, who takes the department of physical science, and by his interesting experiments and lucid descriptions, gives to his listeners an introduction to those departments of knowledge which most abound with illustrations. Last, but far from least, I adore the goodness of

God which sent me so dear and efficient a fellow-helper as my brother in the flesh and in the Lord, J A Spurgeon. His work has greatly relieved me of anxiety, and his superior educational qualifications have tended to raise the tone of the instruction given.

"As to the quality of the preachers whom we have been enabled to send forth, we need no more impartial witness than the good Earl of Shaftesbury, who was kind enough to express himself publicly in Finsbury Chapel, April 4, 1870, in the following generous terms: –

"'It was an utter fallacy to suppose that the people of England would ever be brought to a sense of order and discipline by the repetition of miserable services, by bits of wax candle, by rags of Popery, and by gymnastics in the chancel; nothing was adapted to meet the wants of the people but the Gospel message brought home to their hearts, and he knew of none who had done better service in this evangelistic work than the pupils trained in Mr Spurgeon's College. They had a singular faculty for addressing the population, and going to the very heart of the people.'

"Those who measure effort by result, will be gratified to learn that during the last five years our statistics show that the churches under the care of our young pastors have received a clear increase of TEN THOUSAND MEMBERS. How much of divine power and grace this fact reveals, eternity alone can disclose. Had we had kept records in earlier years we should have seen equal proportionate success; and it is no small matter for rejoicing that the stricter examination of results which we have carried out of late manifests such a satisfactory total.

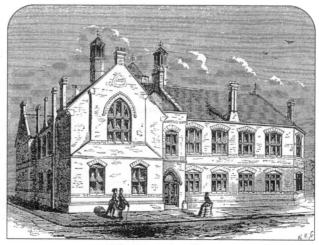

The Pastors' College

"Each year the brethren educated at the Pastors' College are invited to meet in conference at the Tabernacle, and they are generously entertained by our friends. The week is spent in holy fellowship, prayer, and intercourse. By this means men in remote villages, labouring under discouraging circumstances, and ready to sink from loneliness of spirit, are encouraged and strengthened: indeed, all the men confess that a stimulus is thus given which no other means could confer. The Conference of 1870 was regarded by all as a visitation of the Holy Spirit, and the brethren returned to their labour full of zeal and hope.

"All things considered, gratitude and hope are supreme in connection with the Pastors' College, and with praise to God and thanks to a thousand friends, the president and his helpers gird up the loins of their minds for yet more abundant labours in the future. To every land we hope yet to send forth the gospel in its fulness and purity. We pray the Lord to raise up missionaries among our students and make every one a winner of souls. *Brethren, remember this work in your prayers, and in your allotment of the Lord's portion of your substance.*"

Since the above article was written the College has removed from the dark, subterranean rooms under the Tabernacle, into the most convenient, suitable, and commodious new buildings, which have been erected and furnished at the cost of about £15,000, all of which is paid. Here we have a fine hall, excellent classrooms, a handsome library, and in fact all that a College can require. The way in which the money was raised was another instance of divine goodness. £3,000 was given as a memorial to a dear and lamented husband. £2,000 was a legacy to the College from a reader of the sermons. The ministers who had been formerly students came to our help in a princely fashion. Large amounts were made up by the unanimous offerings of Tabernacle friends, on days when the Pastor invited the members and adherents to be his guests at the College. In answer to prayer, the gold and the silver have been ready when needed. How our heart exults and blesses the name of the Lord.

At the present moment (1876) *the Evening Classes* are in a high condition of prosperity, there being about 200 men in regular attendance, and a considerable number among them of hopeful ability. Out of this class City missionaries, lay preachers, writers for the press, and colporteurs, are continually coming. It is an eminently useful part of the College work. These classes have a Loan Library, and contributions of really good, useful books will be gratefully acknowledged.

There are now 330 men proclaiming the gospel in connection with the Baptist denomination who have been trained in the College, of whom two are in India, one in China, two in Spain, one in Rio de Janeiro, one in St Helena, one in Turk's Island, one in South Africa, six in Australia, twenty-three in the United States, and ten in the Canadian Dominion. We are daily expecting more missionaries to be raised up among us; one brother is studying with the Edinburgh Medical Mission, and others who are still in the College have dedicated themselves to Mission work.

Our statistics, which are far from being complete, show that these brethren baptised 20,676 persons in ten years (1865–1874), that the gross increase to their churches was 30,677, and the net increase 19,498. LAUS DEO.

One hundred and twenty pounds will be needed every week to carry on this work. C H Spurgeon, Nightingale Lane, Clapham, Surrey, is the Treasurer.

13
The Stockwell Orphanage

IT would never have occurred to us to commence an Orphanage, but it was a part of the design of Providence that such an institution should form part of our programme, and, therefore, so it is.

In the October number of the *Sword and Trowel* for 1866, there occurs the first allusion to an Orphanage – the fact being that Mrs Hillyard, a devoted sister in the Lord, had put aside £20,000 for this purpose, and invited us to take charge of it. This beloved friend was quite unknown to us until we received a letter intimating her purpose. Our deacons at once agreed to become our co-trustees, and we had a trust deed and scheme prepared. In January, 1867, two-and-a-half acres of ground in Stockwell, abutting upon the Clapham Road, were purchased, and we should have proceeded to build, but a monetary panic occurred, and we were unable to realise the securities which had been handed over to us, which were mainly railway debentures. We could not even pay for the ground without raising a loan on the securities, and this we felt would be a very bad omen at the commencement of the undertaking. The esteemed sister who had so freely given of her substance had invested it very prudently, and it was impossible to foresee the peculiar state of the money market which locked up all our funds; but it was wisely ordered, for the circumstance has been fraught with great results to the Orphanage, since it has compelled us to retain a larger endowment fund than we might otherwise have possessed, if, indeed, we had thought of having any at all.

The scheme of the Orphanage proposed *to do away with all voting and canvassing*, with the wasteful expenditure necessitated thereby, and also *to form the orphans into large families* instead of massing them together upon the workhouse system. This last idea was convenient for the raising of money, for it enabled us to propose that individual donors should each give the amount to build a house, and at the same time we appealed to the Christian public for the means to pay for the land, and the buildings which would be needed for the common use of all the orphans, such as dining hall, schoolrooms, and so on. We carried this matter before God in prayer and looked up, and we beg the reader to follow the entries in the "*Sword and Trowel,*" and mark the goodness of God.

June, 1867 – The Lord is beginning to appear for us in the matter of the Orphanage; but, as yet, he has not opened the windows of heaven as we desire and expect. We wait in prayer and faith. We need no less than £10,000 to erect the buildings, and it will come; for the Lord will answer the prayer of faith. One esteemed friend, Mr George Moore, of Bow Churchyard, has, with spontaneous generosity, sent £250. Three friends have offered £30 each, in the hope that seventeen others will give the same.

July, 1867 – We have been waiting upon the Lord in faith and prayer concerning our Orphanage; but he is pleased at present to try us. As we have no object in view but the glory of God, by the instruction of fatherless boys in the ways of the Lord, having a special view to their souls' salvation, we had hoped that many of the Lord's people would at once have seen the usefulness and practical character of the enterprise, and have sent us substantial aid immediately. The Lord's way, however, is the best, and we rejoice in it, let it be what it may: if the work is to be one of time and long effort, so let it be, if thereby God's name is magnified.

We have engaged a sister to receive the first four orphans into her own hired house until the Orphanages are ready. One beloved friend, the original donor, has given her plate to be sold for this object, and in so doing has set an example to all believers who have surplus silver, which ought to be put to better use than by lying wrapped up in a box.

August, 1867 – Let the facts, which with deep gratitude we record this month, strengthen the faith of believers. In answer to many fervent prayers, the Lord has moved his people to send in during the last month, in different amounts, towards the general funds of the Orphanage, the sum of £1,075, for which we give thanks unto the name of the Lord. More especially do we see the gracious hand of God in the following incidents. A lady who has often aided us in the work of the College, having been spared to see the twenty-fifth anniversary of her marriage-day, her beloved husband presented her with £500 as a token of his ever-growing love to her. Our sister has called upon us, and dedicated the £500 to the building of one of the houses, to be called The Silver Wedding House. The Lord had, however, another substantial gift in store, to encourage us in our work; for a day or two ago a brother beloved in the Lord called upon us on certain business, and when he had retired, he left in a sealed envelope, the sum of £600, which is to be expended in erecting another house. This donation was as little expected as the first, except that our faith expects that all our needs will be supplied in the Lord's own way. The next day, when preaching in the open air, an unknown sister put an envelope into my hand, enclosing £20 for the College, and another £20 for the Orphanage. "What hath God wrought!"

Later on, Mr William Higgs, of the Crown Works, South Lambeth, and his workmen, promised to build a house, and Mr Thomas Olney and sons also agreed to erect another in memory of Mrs Unity Olney, deceased. So things moved on as the Lord would have them do.

The magazine for September, 1867, records the great doings at the laying of the first stones of four houses: the *Silver-wedding House*, by C H S; the *Merchant's House*, by Mrs Hillyard; *Workman's House*, by Mr William Higgs; and *Unity House*, by Mr Thomas Olney, Snr. At the close of the day £2,200 had been brought in: so that the land had been purchased and four houses were provided for without touching Mrs Hillyard's gift. Thus far was the faithfulness of God in answering prayer tried and proved. After the meeting a storm came on and carried away the wooden hall in which the meeting had been held, but the mercy was that this had not happened when we were all assembled in it. The damage was done when no one was injured, and, through the sympathy which it evoked, it was a gain to the funds.

January, 1868 – About three weeks ago, the noble sum of £1,000 was brought us by an unknown gentleman, towards the erection of two other houses.

March, 1868 – Just at the last moment, as we were going to press, we received £2,600 from A B, an unknown friend. We call upon all our friends to magnify the Lord for this amazing instance of his care. How base a thing is unbelief, and how largely does the Lord honour his servants' faith! The note which attended this munificent gift, proves it to be from the same donor who gave £1,000 a few weeks ago. We have feared that the Orphanage might impoverish the College; see, dear readers, how graciously the Lord rebukes this unbelieving fear!

"My dear Sir, – You will remember my intention to send a donation to your College, I have this day dropped into your letter-box an envelope containing two bank notes (£2,000), one of which is for the College and the remaining £1,000 to help complete the Orphanage. The latter led me to contribute to the former. I am a stranger to you but not to your sermons (printed). May the Lord give you health and strength many years to preach his Word, and carry on his work. A B."

April, 1868 – We are proceeding at the Stockwell Orphanage with the schoolroom, dining hall, master's house, four dwelling houses, and the shell of three other houses, which for the present will be used as a hall, in lieu of the erection which was blown down. For all this we look up for means, and means will come.

On June 1st, 1868, the Baptist churches presented £1,200 as a testimonial to C H Spurgeon.

To Messrs. Wigner and Goodall we cannot fully express our sense of obligation, as secretary and treasurer of this fund, which enabled us to build the two houses shown in the engraving, neither can we tell forth the joy which the brotherly love of the churches created in our heart. The amount was afterward made up to £1,765. Upon the splendidly illuminated memorial presented to us were the following kind sentences: –

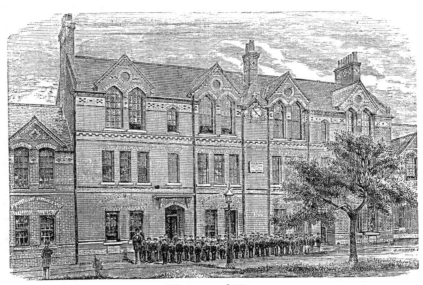

Testimonial House

"To the Rev C H Spurgeon.

"Dear Friend and Brother,

"We have much pleasure in presenting to you herewith a purse containing £1,200, the free-will offerings of a considerable number of individuals and churches of our denomination in the United Kingdom.

"We have a two-fold object in this presentation. First, as a small token of the high esteem in which we hold you; secondly, to aid you in your noble effort to find a home for orphan boys. We have watched your past career with praise and prayer; praise to our covenant-keeping God who has so richly endowed you with gifts for his service, inspired you with zeal in his cause, and blest you with Pentecostal success; prayer, that he would keep you blameless to the end, give you increasing love to and ever-growing success in his kingdom, and, finally, the crown of eternal life. We honour you for your work's sake, nor less for your generous love to all your brethren in the ministry, and to the churches over which they preside. To the blessed God, Father, Son, and Holy Spirit be all the glory.

"We feel a deep interest in the Orphanage scheme which you have been privileged to commence, and pray that you may have all needful grace to carry it on. We desire that the two houses to be built with the money now cheerfully given, may prove an abundant blessing to many sons of good and devoted ministers of Jesus gone to their rest; in them may their children find a precious home, be trained, blest, sanctified, and made blessings – a joy to you and an honour to our Lord.

"We rejoice to be able to say that all the responses to our circular have been most affectionate and hearty, proving the deep interest which the churches feel to the object, how you live in their hearts and are remembered in their prayers.

"Accept, then, dear brother, this testimonial on behalf of all the subscribers, with the assurance of our high esteem, our fervent love, our earnest prayers.

"Grace, mercy and peace be multiplied unto you, through Jesus Christ our Lord.

"We are, dear brother, affectionately yours in Jesus,

"ALEX B GOODALL, *Treasurer*

"JOHN THOMAS WIGNER, *Hon. Sec.*

"1st June, 1868"

On the 19th of June, 1868, on our birthday, we received the tenderest tokens of the love of our dear flock. Mr Thomas Olney, Jnr, and our huge

Sabbath-school, gathered around the first stone of the house which they are to build, and the songs and shouts made us all cheerfully remember our youth. It is no small thing for our esteemed superintendent to undertake to supply a house, but with a little help it will be done. As a token of love from past and present students, they had also resolved to build a house. The Lord bless them for it. Our beloved wife, so long an invalid, and even then far from well, was most lovingly requested by the ministers and students of the College to lay the first stone of the *College House*. She was graciously upheld, although the surpassing kindness displayed was enough to overcome a far stronger frame. After the stone-laying was over, twenty-six sweet little girls in white advanced, one by one, and presented Mrs Spurgeon with purses, which their parents had subscribed as a token of their affectionate rejoicing at her restoration to our midst. It was a most beautiful and unexpected spectacle – one which none will ever forget.

By the end of 1869 all the buildings were finished, at a cost of £10,200, *and were entirely free of debt*. Since then an Infirmary, Bath, and Laundry have been added, and two of the houses have been elevated another storey, and the money has been found for all, by the gracious hand of the Lord.

With 240 children we now need £5,000 per annum; we have constantly received it, and we always shall. The endowments of the institution are now valued at £30,000, and will, we hope, increase until all the expenses will be supplied, and we shall be free to go on to a Girls' Orphanage which we have long contemplated. This story flows on swimmingly, but there have been many trials of faith in the matter, and these continue, so far as the daily expenditure is concerned. A few of our memoranda will show how the Lord delivered us.

December, 1869 – As our friends are aware, we have been suddenly laid aside by an attack of small-pox. When we thus found ourselves put out of the way just when we were wanted in a thousand places, we cried to the Lord to let none of our work suffer, and especially we begged him to care for the Orphanage and College. Within a few hours a beloved friend, knowing nothing of our affliction, called and left £500 for the Orphanage. How condescendingly did the Lord thus ease his poor servant's mind! We felt a sweet peace and holy joy in leaving all the rest of our work in the same hands. A day or two after, Wednesday, November 17, a letter was received, enclosing £1,000. Here again we bless the name of the Lord, and set to our seal that God is true.

October, 1870 – Our best thanks are due to Mr Hugh Stowell Brown, and his friends, for a second time inviting us to Liverpool and giving such noble help to the Orphanage. This makes £450 raised for the Orphans in Myrtle Street.

February, 1871 – Some little time ago, our friend, Mr Bath, who often aids the Orphanage, gave us six dozen bunches of turnips, and merrily added, 'I hope someone will send you the mutton.' About an hour after, a farmer sent a whole sheep; so the mutton and turnips were both on the spot.

One esteemed lady friend, and the ladies of her school, have now made us, we think in all, 700 shirts for the boys. May their labour of love be richly rewarded. (Since then they have sent us in all 2,590 shirts.)

July, 1872 – We have again to sing of mercy. No sooner was the empty state of our Orphanage exchequer made known to our faithful friends, than the Lord inclined their hearts to send the necessary aid. This is a distinct answer to prayer, for other charities have been in the same condition and have made many urgent appeals without evoking the reply which they desired. So prompt and generous have been the responses of our loving helpers, that, after paying £300 for the demands of the month, we have still £1,200 in hand – a marvellous change, indeed, from an actual deficit of £90, and all within a few days.

December, 1873 – We were not well enough to be at the meeting of Trustees, but quite able to understand the report of the monthly settlement. During the week, a friend gave us £50. Mr Chown, of Bradford, kindly sent £125, the result of a collection, and, with other sums, we had more than £700 in hand. The time had, however, come for new suits for the orphans and certain expenses incident to the season, and to our surprise the report of the secretary was, "*All bills paid, but only £3 left.*" Prayer went to work at once, and results followed. Will the reader, however, picture himself with more than 220 boys to feed and £3 in hand! He may say, 'The Lord will provide,' but would he feel the force of this truth if he were in our straits? From the date above mentioned, we have lived on, but it has been very much from hand to mouth – and it is very sweet to see how the Lord provides. A friend in Sweden sent us help, and another from Belgium. A young man sends 6s. 6d., being threepence per week of his first wages, adding, "May it please the Lord to put it into the hearts of many to support you in your great undertaking." A brother, with a large family, offers some potatoes and turnips, and remarks that since he has given to the Orphanage, he has been much the gainer by improved crops. A donor, who is accustomed to store weekly for the Lord, speaks of the plan as greatly beneficial. One who sends a considerable donation, says, "I never write a cheque for you without feeling very sorry that I cannot make it ten times as much." Our expenses, exclusive of our income from property, amount to £10 a day, and two or three gentlemen have each sent us a day's supply; and while the ink is yet in our pen, we are pleasantly interrupted by the postman with two cheques of £10 each from Cardiff. Having soon to start for the south of France, we should be grateful to our heavenly Father if he would enable us to go away with some little store left on hand for the trustees to pay their way with in our absence.

June, 1874 – The funds of the Orphanage ran completely dry on May 8th, and drove us to plead with God for replenishment. The answer was immediate and sufficient. On the very day in which supplication was made nearly £400 was sent into the treasury, and our heart was gladdened.

March, 1875 – The funds of the Orphanage are very low. When the tide has quite ebbed out the flood will return. Our 230 boys persist in eating, and wearing out their clothes, or we would not even mention the matter of failing funds, but appetites are stubborn things, and our boys have double-barrelled ones.

September, 1875 – We have this month received the largest amount, save one, ever entrusted to us at one time, namely £10,000; half of it is for the Orphanage, and will be invested according to our general rule with legacies, unless our daily needs should compel us to draw upon it.

November, 1875 – This month we have had many generous helps, but one of them has charmed us beyond measure. The good friends at Reading have held a bazaar for our Orphanage, and the net result is £1,158! We never dreamed of such a thing, and can hardly realise it now. This is royal munificence, surpassing anything done for us by any town in England. We bless the name of the Lord, and take courage. We can now go away to our short rest without the slightest anxiety on the score of the orphans.

After this manner our experience varies, but never ceases to bear testimony to a faithful God and the power of believing prayer.

The Orphanage is approached from the Clapham Road by a broad avenue, Our woodcut was taken some time ago, and since it was executed,

plane trees have been planted on either side, and have attained a good growth, very greatly adding to the beauty of the entrance. Before you is the entrance arch, to the right is the master's house, and to the left are the dining hall and kitchen. Observe on the pillar on the right the *Sword and the Trowel*, the pastor's motto, and on the left the testimony to the great truth that faith will be honoured and "*The Lord will provide.*" On the inner sides of the two first piers are the text, "*My God shall supply all your need according to his riches in glory by Christ Jesus.*" When standing under the noble archway note again the text which strengthens our hearts in Orphanage work, "*A Father of the fatherless, and a judge of the widow is God in his holy habitation.*" On the piers fronting the Orphanage grounds are the two following inscriptions, "*Solomon in all his glory was not arrayed like one of these,*" and, "*Your heavenly Father feedeth them,*" which again proclaim our hope and the ground of our confidence.

On looking from under the arch the visitor is struck with the size and beauty of the buildings, and the delightfully airy and open character of the whole institution. It is a place of sweetness and light, where merry voices ring out and happy children play. The stranger will be pleased with *the dining hall*, hung round with engravings given by Mr Graves, of Pall Mall; he will be shown into *the board room* where the trustees transact the business: and he will be specially pleased with *the great play hall* in which our public meetings are held and the boys'

Stockwell Orphanage

sports are carried on. There is the swimming bath, which enables us to say that nearly every boy can swim. Up at the very top of the buildings, after ascending two flights of stairs, the visitor will find the *schoolrooms*, which from their very position are airy and wholesome. The floors, scrubbed by the boys themselves, the beds made, and the domestic arrangements all kept in order by their own labour, are usually spoken of with approbation. The matrons are glad to show friends over their houses; Mr Charlesworth, the excellent master, is always pleased to arrange for friends to look over the schools and the buildings, and when there is no contagious disease abroad, he will conduct them to the *Infirmary*, where the best of nurses will be glad to show them their domains.

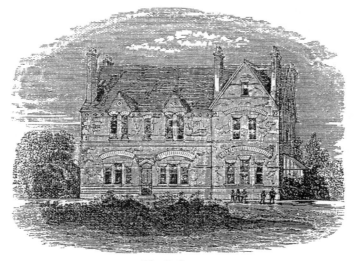

The Infirmary

The Infirmary itself stands at the further end of the Orphanage grounds, and is spacious enough to accommodate a large number of children should an epidemic break out in the institution. It was built after the other portions had been finished, and has proved a great blessing, for ever since its erection, the speedy isolation of ailing boys has checked the spread of contagious disease, and by God's blessing has preserved our average of health at a very high point indeed. We give a view of it above.

Our esteemed friend, Mr Charlesworth, formerly assistant minister at Surrey Chapel, enters most heartily into his work, and as headmaster saves us a world of anxiety. We are also singularly happy in all the helpers. Long may they be spared to us. We are under deep obligations to Messrs. Bartlett, Daniel, Evans, Macgregor, Andrew Dunn, and others, who labour for the spiritual good of the boys on the Sabbath, and to voluntary teachers who kindly take such branches of education as French, Music, and so on, and give us their services without fee or reward. Inasmuch as these, and our donors, and various helpers have done it unto these little ones, they have done it unto their Lord himself, and they shall not lack their reward.

We have already seen many children converted, and these are formed into a Christian band. Several of the lads who have left have subscribed handsomely to the funds; almost without exception all the boys in situations are doing well, and one is in the College, giving every token of becoming a good minister of Jesus Christ.

The whole work is carried on in dependence upon God, and his blessing is manifestly resting upon it. Having no list of subscribers, no payments for votes, and a continual need for nearly £4,000 above the income from property, we are, nevertheless, well supplied. At the same time, as the Lord works by means, the reader will, we trust, consider how much of the needed provision he is himself bound to send in. About £80 a week is needed. Gifts of food, clothing, firing, and so on, will be acceptable. Direct cash to C H Spurgeon, Nightingale Lane, Clapham, Surrey, and parcels to Mr Charlesworth, the Orphanage, Stockwell. The Orphanage is for destitute fatherless boys. Applicants must be between the ages of six and ten.

14
The Colportage Association

ALTHOUGH in order of time the Colportage was our third work, we are very far from considering it to be of third-rate importance; on the contrary, we believe it to be one of the most efficient and economical agencies in existence, and, as education increases, it will be more and more so. The sale of vicious literature can only be met by the distribution of good books: these can only be scattered in rural districts by carrying the books to the doors, and even in towns the book-hawkers' work greatly stimulates their sale. Scotland has long had a grand staff of colporteurs, it was time to make a beginning for England.

The work was forced upon us by the earnestness of a generous friend at the Tabernacle to whom we are under great obligations. The committee was formed in September, 1866: certain earnest young brethren undertaking the management of the enterprise. During the next two years *six* men were employed, and it was not easy to find the means for their support; this enterprise seemed to be one plant too many in our garden, and had it not been for the persevering entreaties of the principal promoter of this work, we should have allowed it to die out. In 1872 the work began to grow, and God's good hand was with it, so that thirteen men were in the field. This growth rendered it needful to supplement the energetic labours of the honorary staff, to whom great honour is due, by appointing a paid secretary, Mr W Corden Jones, who has proved to be well adapted to his place. In 1874 the sales had nearly reached £3,000, with thirty-five men at work, and at this moment (1876) forty-five men are employed. The Society now possesses a trade stock of £800, and is in need of an annual income of £2,500. These dimensions are respectable, but to meet the demands of England they ought to be multiplied by ten.

The depot of this society is in the College buildings. The society is unsectarian in principle, after the same manner as the London City Mission; although most of its colporteurs are Baptists at present, this arises from the fact that they have been applied for by Baptists and supported by them. Each man costs about £80 per annum, but on the receipt of £40 a year from any lovers of a full and free salvation, a colporteur will be appointed to the district which the donors may select, and the colporteur will work in connection with those who provide this measure of support. Many churches find such a man to be the best and cheapest worker imaginable.

The Colporteur

The colporteur not only endeavours to sell books, but he visits from door to door, and in so doing converses with the people about their souls, prays with the sick, and leaves a tract at each cottage. He is frequently able to hold prayer meetings, open air services, and Bible-readings. He gets a room, if possible, and preaches, founds Bands of Hope, and makes himself generally useful in the cause of religion and temperance. He is in fact at first a missionary, then a preacher, and by-and-bye in the truest sense a pastor. We have some noble men in this work. All are not equally good, some have even proved slothful; but the system is one which soon discovers a man's negligence, since his sales fall off, and the monthly report tells the tale.

The book-hawker stands upon a vantage ground as a house to house missionary. His pack is a passport to every door, the attempt to sell is an opportunity for declaring the Gospel, and the book itself is a ready text. When we think of 300,000 visits paid in one year among a priest-ridden peasantry, we are encouraged, and give God the glory. But we cannot restrain the sigh: "O that some rich stewards of the Lord would look on this work and help us to increase it." London has only one of our colporteurs and yet needs them badly; how is this? Will no one employ a man? No money can be more wisely expended, nor used more directly for the benefit of those who most require it. Send on your cheques to C H Spurgeon, Nightingale Lane, Clapham, Surrey. Reports and every information will be cheerfully sent on application to the Secretary of the Colportage Society, Pastors' College, Temple Street, Southwark.

Bible Carriage

Mr Charlesworth's two Bible-classes have generously agreed to support a brother with a Bible carriage in the streets of London. Would not some other communities of young people do well to have their own man at work in the regions where they dwell? THINK OF IT.

15
Other Institutions Connected with the Tabernacle

Tabernacle Building Fund – Up to January 1876, this fund stood at £4,300, but by the generous offer of an anonymous donor it has just now been raised to £5,000. The capital is lent out without interest to chapels in debt, to encourage them to clear themselves of their liabilities. Thus this capital remains and continues to benefit one church after another. The fund was originally raised in order that the Pastor might feel that in case of his death there would be money available to pay for the completion of the studies of the men in College: to do this, however, would now require a large amount.

Mrs Spurgeon's Book Fund – The Pastor's beloved wife, touched with the poverty of many ministers, commenced this fund to supply the most needy with books. She makes this the pleasant business of her life, when she has respite from pain, and sufficient strength. Already (March, 1876) she has received and expended £300, having by prudent purchasing been able to give at least £500 worth of books to brethren whose libraries are scantily furnished.

Mr Oncken's German Mission – The church supports two missionaries in Germany – at Templin and Hamburg.

Mission to the Jews – There is a small auxiliary to this mission, of which Miss Higgs is the secretary.

Mr Orsman's Mission in Golden Lane, City, one of the most useful in all London, is an entirely independent enterprise, but Mr Orsman, as still a member at the Tabernacle, would be unhappy if we did not mention him. All the arrangements of an active church, and all the necessary adjuncts of a vigorous mission, are to be found under the supervision of this honoured brother, who deserves all the encouragement and assistance that can be rendered him.

Richmond Street Mission and Schools, Walworth. President J T Dunn – In 1875 new premises were erected for this mission at a cost of over £900 which is all paid. Sunday and Ragged Schools, and adult classes. Children in schools 650. Preaching, tract distribution, Band of Hope, Evangelistic work, etc, – all in active operation.

Green Walk Mission, Bermondsey – President, W Olney, Jnr. A mighty warfare against sin has been carried on here, and very many brought to Jesus and added to the Tabernacle church. Hall thronged to hear the gospel. About 850 children in the schools. Mothers meetings, Band of Hope, Tract Society, Open air mission, Bible and singing classes, and Children's special service. All at work and all alive. *Here a good hall must be built.* If some generous friend would build a place for this mission, the money would be well laid out.

James Grove, Peckham – Here a chapel has been built and a congregation gathered, with schools. Our Elder, John Field, has just left it for a pastorate, and matters are in a transition state. It is a fine property, and much good has been done in it. Many members have been added to the Tabernacle church, and we hope before long to form them into a separate community, and let them run alone.

Mr Hampton's Mission – Established four years, for the evangelisation of the poor blind. For this we need a hall, for at present we are cramped for numbers, and the overcrowding of very poor people is most unhealthy, and indeed unbearable. There is a Sunday School for blind children. Tea is given on Sunday afternoon to the blind and their guides, and then service is held. Two hundred blind and guides attend. £148 expended in 1875, and much more is needed: but a hall near the Tabernacle is our greatest necessity. Remittances can be sent to C H Spurgeon, president. Mr Hampton, a working painter, is the right worthy conductor of this work of mercy.

Mrs Thomas's Mothers' Mission – Our afflicted friend carries on this work with the help of some of our members, and it is a great success. Seventy women are on the books. £70 expended per annum. Clothes, loan-boxes, and so on, provided for poor women.

Other mothers' meetings are held by various ladies of the church.

Tabernacle Sunday School – Superintendent, Mr Davis. Held in the Tabernacle schoolroom and in the College. Children, 1,000 in regular attendance; 150 in senior classes, which each one deserve separate mention if we had space; 37 joined the church in 1875. Young Christians' Association, 216 members. Children's and teachers' Library. The school raises from £50 to £60 per annum for the Baptist Missionary Society. There is a Band of Hope, and a working class.

Almshouses – The day schools are as full as they can hold, and under Mr Johnson's care provide a superior education. Here there are Sunday Schools, and an adult class of 120 members under Mr Daniel. Mr Bartlett's children's service is held in the evening, and he also conducts a young Christians' meeting.

Orphanage: here, too, Sunday School work goes on vigorously.

Several schools in our neighbourhood are wholly conducted and many more very nearly so by our members, but as they nominally belong to other churches, or are quite independent, we do not mention them here, though we furnish teachers for schools all around us.

Mrs Bartlett's Class – This famous class, since the decease of its invaluable leader, is now presided over by her son Edward, who is an indefatigable labourer in many ways. The class is well attended, numbering from 500 to 700; it carries on many meetings and works of usefulness, and manifests a right royal liberality to the College, for which it raises a large amount annually. Very many have come into the church from this class.

Mr Perkins' Bible Class – An earnest, united band of young men, who meet on Sabbath afternoons in the Vestry of the Tabernacle. They carry on different works of usefulness and aid the College.

Mr Bowker's Bible Class is of the same character, and meets in the Octagonal Room of the College. It is an earnest class, helps its own poor, works for Jesus, and aids in supporting the College.

Mr Charlesworth has a Ladies' Bible Class, on Thursdays before the service, and a *Young Men's Bible Class on* Sabbath afternoons – both prospering. The two classes support a Bible-carriage.

Baptist Country Mission – President, Mr Bowker. A small society, but full of life. It seeks to evangelise the villages by open air preaching and opening rooms for services. With small funds, it has during the last year carried on three promising interests – in Putney, Walthamstow, and Carshalton. Others in past years have become self-supporting churches, and so will these. It is making attempts in villages further afield, and Christ is preached faithfully. It is an evangelistic effort for the suburbs and country. Its expenditure was only £60 last year. It could economically use ten times as much.

Evangelist's Association – Secretary, Elder Elvin. Is fully at work in halls, lodging-houses, street corners, the Tabernacle steps, etc. Services have been successfully carried on at Dunn's Institute, and Tabernacle Almshouses, and in various chapels where the ministers have allowed evangelistic meetings to be held. This society sends brethren to any church needing such assistance. Expenses in 1875, £40.

Loan Tract Society for Tabernacle District – Secretary, Mr Wood. Tracts and the pastor's sermons are lent out and 2,000 families visited every week. Several conversions have resulted.

General Loan Tract Society – Secretary, Mr Cornell. Supplies the pastor's sermons in free grants to poor districts, where friends arrange for their loan. With the very best results this work has been carried on in seventeen counties of England, and had we more money and more applicants this agency would become a great power. Income £45.

Another Society, called *The Rock Loan Tract Society*, lends sermons chiefly in country villages. Secretary, Mr Hawkins.

The Ordinance Poor Fund distributes among the poor members of the church about £800 annually.

Ladies' Benevolent Society – Secretary, Mrs Potier. For making clothing, and relieving the poor. A very useful society. Income £105.

Ladies' Maternal Society – Secretary, Mrs Jenkins. For the aid of poor women in their confinements. 162 boxes of linen lent during the year. Income £56. A society which ought to be seven times as large.

Mrs Evans' Home and Foreign Missionary Working Society makes up boxes of garments for missionaries, and also for poor ministers and their families at home. This is a blessed work, and has made glad many a poor servant of Jesus. Friends who wish to aid poor Baptist ministers cannot do better than give their money to this society, which, by the willing work of its young members, turns the money into useful articles.

Two *Benefit Societies* hold their meetings in the rooms of the Tabernacle – "The United Christian Brothers," and "The United Christian Sisters." For the payment of 6d. per week, 10s. a week is provided in sickness, and £10 at death of a member or member's wife. These societies are not a part of the church work, but we believe that they do much good.

Addendum

1884 marked C H Spurgeon's 50th birthday and special services were held. During the course of those meetings Spurgeon's secretary, Mr Harrald, read a list to the congregation of the many facets of the work at the Metropolitan Tabernacle at the time represented by societies run and staffed by its members. The following extract is from those proceedings:

C H SPURGEON: Now I am going to ask Mr Harrald to read the list of societies represented here tonight. I think everybody should know what the church has been moved to do, and I beg to say that there are other societies besides those which will be mentioned, but you will be tired before you get to the end of them.

Mr J W HARRALD read the following list: –

The Almshouses;
The Pastors' College;
The Pastors' College Society of Evangelists;
The Stockwell Orphanage;
The Colportage Association;
Mrs Spurgeon's Book Fund, and Pastors' Aid Fund;
The Pastors' College Evening Classes;
The Evangelists' Association;
The Country Mission;
The Ladies' Benevolent Society;
The Ladies' Maternal Society;
The Poor Ministers' Clothing Society;
The Loan Tract Society;
Spurgeon's Sermons' Tract Society;
The Evangelists' Training Class;
The Orphanage Working Meeting;
The Colportage Working Meeting;
The Flower Mission;
The Gospel Temperance Society;
The Band of Hope;
The United Christian Brothers' Benefit Society;
The United Christian Sisters' Benefit Society;
The Young Christians' Association;
The Mission to Foreign Seamen;
The Mission to Policemen;
The Coffee-House Mission;

The Metropolitan Tabernacle Sunday School;
Mr Wigney's Bible Class;
Mr Hoyland's Bible Class;
Miss Swain's Bible Class;
Miss Hobbs' Bible Class;
Miss Hooper's Bible Class;
Mr Bowker's Bible Class for Adults of both Sexes;
Mr Dunn's Bible Class for Men;
Mrs Allison's Bible Class for Young Women;
Mr Bartlett's Bible Class for Young Women;
Golden Lane and Hoxton Mission (Mr Orsman's);
Ebury Mission and Schools, Pimlico;
Green Walk Mission and Schools,
Haddon Hall;
Richmond Street Mission and Schools;
Flint Street Mission and Schools;
North Street, Kennington, Mission and Schools;
Little George Street Mission, Bermondsey;
Snow's Fields Mission, Bermondsey;
The Almhouses Missions;
The Almshouses Sunday Schools;
The Almshouses Day Schools;
The Townsend Street Mission;
The Townley Street Mission;
The Deacon Street Mission;
The Blenheim Grove Mission, Peckham;
The Surrey Gardens Mission;
The Vinegar Yard Mission, Old Street;
The Horse Shoe Wharf Mission and Schools;
The Upper Ground Street Mission;
The Thomas Street Mission, Horsleydown;
The Boundary Row Sunday School, Camberwell;
The Great Hunter Street Sunday School, Dover Road;
The Carter Street Sunday School, Walworth;
The Pleasant Row Sunday Schools, Kennington;

The Westmoreland Road Sunday Schools, Walworth;

The Lansdowne Place Sunday School;

Miss Emery's Banner Class, Brandon Street;

Miss Miller's Mothers' Meeting;

Miss Ivimey's Mothers' Meeting;

Miss Francies' Mothers' Meeting.

C H SPURGEON: We have need to praise God that he enables the church to carry on all these institutions. [1]

---

1. Such a list is a rebuke to present-day inactivity in reformed churches. Spurgeon, an avowed believer in Sovereign Grace, saw no inconsistency in encouraging fervent activity throughout the church alongside the preaching of the Gospel in seeking to reach "every creature." – MPR.

BV - #0078 - 110624 - C0 - 234/156/8 - PB - 9781788722667 - Gloss Lamination